DR. JOY BROWNE

Why They Don't Call

When They Say They Will

...and Other Mixed

Signals

SIMON AND SCHUSTER
NEW YORK LONDON TORONTO
SYDNEY TOKYO

Simon and Schuster
Simon & Schuster Building
Rockefeller Center
1230 Avenue of the Americas
New York, New York 10020

Designed by Kathy Kikkert
Manufactured in the United States of America

10 9 8 7 6 5 4 3 2 1

Library of Congress Cataloging in
Publication Data

Browne, Joy, 1944–
    Why they don't call when they say they will—and other
mixed signals / Joy Browne.
        p.   cm.
    1. Courtship—United States. 2. Dating (Social
customs) 3. Sex differences (Psychology) 4. Interpersonal
conflict—United States. 5. Intimacy (Psychology) I. Title.
HQ801.B87   1989   89–11462
306.73'4—dc20   CIP

ISBN 0-671-67532-X

Acknowledgments

♥

For a psychologist, life is the lab and nearly everything and everyone is suitable for study and analysis. My friends and coworkers have been reassured up to this point that I "only do it for money," i.e., put on my shrink hat. They have believed it because I have believed it, and it is only now that I am beginning to realize I may do it only for money, but it's stored for free, able to be brought forth at the drop of a word processor. Because this book is so much more personal than any I have written (or am likely to write in the near future) more of you may recognize yourselves. The intention was always to illuminate the issue, not the personality, but if I have come a bit too close for comfort, please forgive me and accept that I really did write this book in response to your dilemmas, hurts, tears, giggles, and 2 A.M. phone calls. It is only as I am writing this that I understand how much I value, appreciate, and am indebted to your candor and trust in me.

My most heartfelt and held-breath gratitude to you guys, my friends and coworkers who have helped me to understand how men and women REALLY feel, not how we're supposed to or should or could. My hope is that your aches may be lessened by the realization that it's not just you and that you're not alone. I suppose the significant men in my life—you do know who you are, don't you?—also deserve a hug. Again, if things seem a bit close to the bone, I won't tell if you won't.

In saying thank you to good buddies, my editor Nancy Nicholas deserves to be noted by name since she has served as the bridge between the candor of my friends and the anticipated glare of publicity on their tales. Serving as censor, confidante, teller of tales, and calmer of nerves, she protects us all.

Saying thanks to a machine seems absurd, especially given the nature of the very personal thanks involved in this book, but my little word processor makes things LOOK so much neater that I probably got some things past Nancy that never would have flown on my Selectric and Erasable bond combo.

If we can walk a calm, comfortable mile in one another's argyles or pantyhose, maybe we can make the world a warmer, gentler, happier place for men and women, and all my 2 A.M. phone calls will be about triumphs and engagements and warmth and wonder.

To Mom,
who told me that boys and girls
were just the same,
and my daughter,
who has been trying to convince me
that they're not . . .
I love you both.

Contents

♥

CONTENTS

Introduction

♥

Men and women are different. They look different, they act different, they may even think differently. They use the same words to mean different things. Whether these differences are biological and inherent or the result of gender-related upbringings in a culture that ascribes almost opposite meanings to the same behavior depending on the sex of the actor doesn't really matter. The point is they are different, he and she. About the only thing they both do the same is seemingly effortlessly misunderstand each other and blame the other for the mess that is often the result of men and women simply trying to get together—from the very earliest first timid missteps to the final misunderstandings and beyond. . . .

The book explains the blame game: what happens (the game), the results (the blame), the misunderstandings (the explanation), and how to avoid the whole mess next time should there ever be a next time (the resolution).

Unless either he or she is opting for the monastic life, this understanding should save a lot of wear and tear in terms of future hassles, make-up presents, hurt feelings, and a small fortune in long distance phone calls and lawyers' fees.

At a time when people seemingly are looking for permanency in their personal relationships to a degree unprecedented in the last quarter of a century, this book is an attempt to understand and acknowledge the differences between men and women which seem to loom larger than ever before. Once both partners are willing to start admitting that they might not share a perspective, each one can work toward strengthening and enhancing the interaction rather than fighting over who is right or misguided or malicious or stupid or just plain uninterested. The very stuff of disagreement can then be turned into enlarged and valuable insight.

The game is the same, men and women together, but the rules have altered in terms of what each wants and is willing to offer the other. By acknowledging these differences, both historical and contemporary, solutions that are mutually satisfying, fair, and reasonable can be reached, based on these very real variations, and without resorting to blame.

Men aren't the enemy nor are women, but we've been brought up to think about ourselves and each other in such disparate ways that it's easy to get angry at these often opposite points of view, not to mention behavior. The times and the rules between the sexes are changing, but that doesn't mean that there are good guys and bad guys, just messy situations that confuse both parties.

Both sexes are more distrustful of the other's motives than ever before. (MEN: All they want is somebody rich to take care of them, buy them presents, provide a lifestyle and an escort service, a stud service if need be for fun or babies. And they want us to be sensitive but not wimpy, strong but not macho, caring but not possessive. What's in it for me??) (WOMEN: The good ones are married, gay, bastards, wimps, or some combination of the above. They are all little boys who want a bimbo version of their mothers.)

Our society may have raised sexual blame to an art form as an unfortunate side effect of the women's movement. Women blame men for their oppression; men blame women for their impotence. We've had a quarter of a century to get the rhetoric shined and polished to the extent that most swallow the perspective, hook, line, and sinker. A serious, pervasive problem does indeed exist as does the heartfelt, urgent wish for a solution.

This book isn't about turning back the clock to a gentler time or erasing the last twenty years of the collective consciousness; it is about understanding what makes men and women tick, sometimes in sync, often to the beat of completely different metronomes.

Why Don't They Call When They Say They Will . . . is about breaking the code, understanding the clues, symbols, words, looks. It's about the hidden and misleading, the uninterpreted and the misinterpreted. It's about looking for some of the trouble spots most likely to occur between two adults, given that one of them has been raised male and the other female. This book is not about blaming one sex or the other, nor is it about anger toward parents, or about limitations, expectations, or shortages of suitable partners. It is about being realistic about who you are and what you want, the distinction between wanting and needing someone or something, and distinguishing between emotions and thoughts. It will also be a lot about some of the seemingly trivial problems that occur between men and women that make very little sense but an inordinate amount of trouble.

This is a dating, not a marriage, manual and it is intended for use by relatively sane adults who are looking for relatively sane, grown-up adult relationships but who don't seem to have quite gotten the knack yet.

The scenarios presented are both common and avoidable. I will discuss the differences in male and female perceptions, behaviors, assumptions, socialization, and goals—from the initial encounter, which could be as brief as a glance across the room, to the preliminary overture (Haven't I seen you somewhere before?) to the initial contact (perhaps a request for a phone number) through the first conversation, initial intentional encounter (better known in the vernacular as the first date), through stages of communication (or lack thereof), consummation evolving into a first stage commitment eventually evolving into a longer term arrangement that either continues or dissolves. In addition, I will show how change within the context of any existing understanding affects both parties whether the change is forward, backward, or to another stage.

This is often a clear if intense arena in which differences are obvious. Those differences can depend on such variables as who makes the overtures, why and how they are made, not to mention how your momma raised you.

As uncomfortable as many of these games seem, they focus on the similarities and differences between men and women and the real if uncomfortable possibility there might be room for one to change, adjust, and even profit from the previous seemingly insurmountable barriers between the sexes. And they suggest this might be possible without destroying one's self, the other person, or the relationship. Alteration without destruction is a possibility once differences are understood and taken into account.

Men and women continue to be drawn together, but with a bit more insight into self and other in terms of both behavior and thought processes—the magnetism can be a bit more blamefree, less embittered, and more fun. The games discussed will include the phone call, girl time vs. boy time, flowers, friends, first date, sex, lying, restaurants, commitment, relatives, leftover kids, weddings (yours and others'), confidentiality, old flames, confessions, infidelity, security, kids, housework, affection, meals, anniversaries, talking, birthdays, vacations, flirting, binges, the guys, free time, sexual experimentation, money, commitment, power, control, and cars.

A glossary will be included at the end which is a sort of tongue-in-cheek shorthand way of summarizing the different world views of men and women.

Phone Numbers

THE GAME

They have met at a friend's party and have spent most of the evening chatting. Her ride is now ready to leave. She tells him she has really enjoyed talking with him. He smiles and says, "I'd like to call you—may I have your phone number?" She delightedly gives it to him, kisses him on the cheek, and leaves. On the way home, she tells her girlfriend how neat he is, how much she likes his sense of humor, and she wonders whether he will have called by the time she reaches home. For the next week, she checks her answering machine twice an hour, has the phone company check her phone twice during the week, and avoids spending more than two minutes at a time on the phone for fear he will get a busy signal and give up. By the middle of the second week, she has confided in her best friend that she wasn't all that crazy about him, and by the end of the second week, she just wants the creep to call so she can have the satisfaction of telling him that she would never in a million years go out with somebody like him.

THE BLAME

HE feels that asking a woman for her phone number is the only possible polite way to end a conversation. He would never openly insult a woman by *not* asking. He hasn't really thought about whether he would like to see her again, but he's up to his eyeballs at work and is currently dating a perfectly nice woman who happened to be out of town the night he met our currently anguished she.

SHE feels that all men are basically predators out to notch their belt with women's smiles, phone numbers, hopes, and pelts. This attitude is as much a result of as a cause of her currently lonely state. She had already figured out what she was going to say when he called, what she was going to wear on their first date, and the color of their living-room furniture. She somehow assumed that he was different and is embittered by his callousness. She feels hurt and rejected and duped and yet is terrified that if he ever does call, she might just be desperate enough to go out with the bum. She's angry with herself for getting sucked in again, yet this time she was so sure. . . .

THE EXPLANATION

After initial contact, the phone is probably the most treacherous obstacle to a happy relationship. It looms larger than sex, old lovers, miscellaneous leftover spouses, kids, pets, and religious differences. It's not that all of these won't come into play, it's just that you have to get by the first telephone call to be driven to distraction by anything else. Unfortunately this encounter has followed the common, time-honored tradition in which the male asks for the female's phone number and she has to decide whether or not to give it to him. And so the whole mess begins.

Waiting by the phone and nervous checks on the answering machine become a way of life. If he hasn't called immediately, she gets more and more anxious, and finally decides she has found just another in a long line of disappointing males vindicating her long-held belief that all men are thoughtless, inconsiderate bastards. If he finally does call, he is likely to be met with a seething wall of hostility. How does this mess come to pass, and how can it be avoided?

THE RESOLUTION

Once we accept the ritual that a man feels he *has* to say "Can I call you?" rather than "Good night" or "I'm married" or "You're nice, but not my type," it is inevitable that he will ask for and usually will receive a phone number. Even the most cynical female assumes that this time this guy really will call. Why else would he ask? She has already forgotten not only all previous experiences to the contrary, but that it isn't really much trouble for him to ask. Female hormones at work, demonstrating the power of hope over experience.

A logical approach to this dilemma would be to change the rules—to make it customary for the *woman* to get the *man's* phone number. Why hasn't this occurred to more couples or would-be couples? Because women still want to be courted, and men like to feel in charge. Hence, there are a lot of angry, passive, tense people, waiting and wanting to be pursued. It's not only conditioning but biological destiny that dictates that women demand emotional security before submitting sexually, emotionally, socially. And even today, most women and men feel that if a woman takes the initiative, she is more sexually available; she is acting like a "man" and therefore must want what a man "wants," and we all know what a man wants, wink, wink. All of which gets us right back to the security issue again.

Men, for heaven's sake, *don't* ask for a phone number unless you really think you might call. This means that you have to be aware of your intentions earlier than is your habit. Parties may be for loosening up, but if you can maintain some self-control and sobriety, chemical, bio-chemical, and emotional, you may save a lot of wear and tear on your own conscience and some gullible, infatuated female. If you can't do it for your own ethical well-being, do it for the good of all mankind, and I do mean *man*kind. You're not doing yourself or your brothers any good by embittering one more female. If you're not going to call, don't get a number. If you're going to call, do it within three or four days, or leave a message explaining that you're going to be out of town, that you're going through a personal crisis, that your divorce isn't final—whatever will communicate your real message: "I'm attracted to you, but I was a little less than forthcoming about my current availability." This will allow her to get herself off your hook.

Women, stop being so dopey. Instead of giving out your phone number, take his and call him if you want to. He can court you later on the *second* date. By then, you can decide whether to give him your phone number. Worst case is that you give him your number and he doesn't call, but you still have his number, so you can call him if you want. At least you're not sitting around waiting for the phone to ring, feeling anxious, angry, and stupid.

Don't worry about his possible assumption that you're sexually available, since you've taken the initiative. You're a big girl. You can explain that you were just being friendly, not necessarily coming on to him. You haven't lost the right to say no. Anyway, the trade-off is between agonizing passivity and eventual confrontation. Go for it. Think of all the anxiety you won't suffer, all the times you won't have to check your machine.

This doesn't mean that you should start acting like an inconsiderate man, collecting phone numbers you have no real intention of dialing. You may find that playing this game gives you an enormous sense of power—but do you really want to inflict the pain you have experienced on someone who's only sin is showing some interest in you?

First Date

THE GAME

Mutual friends had suggested that they would really enjoy each other, so he had called her and they had arranged for a dinner and movie the coming Wednesday night. She had her hair done and bought a new dress, desperate to make a good impression. He took her to a foreign movie, because he thought Clint Eastwood wasn't her style, and then to a local restaurant that had stopped serving ten minutes before they arrived. They settled for drinks on an empty stomach. He made a halfhearted pass so the evening wouldn't turn out to be a total loss. She was miffed as much by the low-rent evening as by his putting a move on her, and a feeble one at that. By the end of the date both were hungry, grumpy, a little drunk, and completely disappointed in their friends as matchmakers.

THE BLAME

HE felt that she was just one more woman who was interested in a fancy, free dinner. She never relaxed, never just had a good time. Okay, maybe he should have found out how late the restaurant served and what time the movie ended and what the critics thought of it, but hey, no big deal. This was just a chance to get to know each other, and she certainly wasn't much of a sport. And besides, why was it all his problem anyway?

SHE isn't crazy about being treated with such indifference. She went to all the trouble of getting her hair done and buying a new dress, and he wasn't even willing to spring for dinner. He seems to be an incompetent nerd, and then to top things off, after never even holding her hand during the evening, he made a move on her after getting liquored up. What a spoiled, take-everything-for-granted male chauvinist pig. And Wednesday night for a date—as though she weren't good enough for a weekend night. Pleeeze.

THE EXPLANATION

First dates are the pits and blind dates are first dates from hell. Our own expectations, societal rules, the things our mothers told us, pressure from friends—everything makes first dates scary. Ideally, all dates should start with the fourth or fifth encounter. Even when you know somebody beforehand, that first official date can be a killer. The fact that these two had never even set eyes on each other only made a bad situation worse.

SHE was trying too hard to look perfect and be agreeable and be the woman she thought he wanted her to be. She's angry with herself for agreeing to go to a movie on a first date. (How can anybody get to know anybody else in a movie? Talking at movies is, or should be, strictly forbidden!) Her powerlessness is societally enforced and culturally determined, but that doesn't mean that she has to buy it so completely. If she had lowered her expectations, made less initial fuss, allowed herself to relax, been less determined to please, she might have had less to be angry about. She feels victimized, but she placed herself in the role of victim. Interviewing for a prospective spouse on a first date is a waste of time and energy. She cared too much.

HE appeared to care too little. His nonchalance bordered on rudeness and at very least exhibited a lack of planning. The need to appear cool is probably responsible for more rotten first dates than personality mismatches and zits put together and multiplied by ten. Instead of trying to impress her with his worldly nonchalance, he might have opted for a shorter, maybe even daytime, limited, face-to-face interaction. A walk in the park, a trip to a museum, brunch—any occasion that allowed for low key interaction would have better served his purpose to get to know her. A movie is a crutch that allows some physical closeness without the need to talk and in theory something to talk about when the lights go on. But it is a better ploy after some contact has been made.

THE RESOLUTION

First dates will probably always be one of those things that rank just above food poisoning on anybody's wish list. They have to occur for any subsequent date to occur, but their negative impact can be limited by keeping in

mind that the whole purpose is to allow the two participants to get to know each other a bit. This means the
surroundings should be nonthreatening and the stakes
low enough so both people can feel free to be their worst
selves and get it all out of the way, or can at least not
have to be their best selves. Old-fashioned dating is
really an upside-down experience in that each person is
on his or her best behavior, best clothes, best manners
up front, and then gradually lets down the guard and
becomes more real, at which point the other person is
shocked at the transformation. We should be our most
real selves up front when the stakes are low. Instead,
women try to be their most agreeable and men try to be
their coolest.

Women might also try less hard if they did more of
the asking, so they would feel less passive. That doesn't
mean they have to adopt the ultimate Joe Cool role but
they would have less responsibility to please. Admittedly one of the reasons that men are still allowed to
take the first step and that meals are still so much a part
of the scenario is that it's one of the last situations in
which men can still comfortably nurture women. Maybe
we need to find other ways and places to help everybody's digestion.

First dates become much more useful when we view
them as opportunities for information gathering, rather
than auditions. Women need to care less about appearing to be compliant, and men need to care less about
appearing terminally suave, cool, and uninterested.
Then some real business might get accomplished.

Girl Time and Boy Time

♥

THE GAME

They've had a wonderful dinner together, talked the evening away, gone dancing, and ended up back at her front door. They both have early-morning meetings, so with obvious regret, he sweetly kisses her good night, murmuring, "I'll call you soon." She drifts on clouds into her nightie and brushes her teeth, keeping half an ear cocked, halfway expecting the phone to ring because he has impetuously decided to call from a phone booth on the way home to tell her how terrific she is. Her phone is silent, and not only for the night; she doesn't hear from him at work or that evening nor the next. He finally calls a week later and is met with an iciness bordering on rudeness, and an implacable refusal to go out with him again.

THE BLAME

HE is profoundly confused. He really likes her and was looking forward to seeing her again. They seemed to have an easy, relaxed time together, and she seemed fun and undemanding. Her coldness is baffling. He can only assume that she is one of those teases who likes to see whom she can ensnare and then dump; that she has a boyfriend and was just fooling around on the side; that someone better came along; or that upon reflection she's decided he's not rich enough (or handsome or sexy or worldly or interesting enough); or that she's having her period; or that she's mildly emotionally disturbed and should probably be avoided like the plague. He already has tangled with enough women who have unpredictable mood swings.

SHE is furious. One more inconsiderate, lousy, self-involved spoiled male who feels that women are just falling all over themselves to be with him. Who the hell does he think he is? He says he'll call soon and then plays this dumb game. He must think she's really hard up. She's sure that if she's dumb enough to go out with him, he'll pull the same stunt over and over again, showing her how unimportant she is and how important he is. She's been there before, thank you very much, and doesn't need to do this number again.

THE EXPLANATION

Einstein said time is relative, and he didn't know the half of it. It's not only relative, it's sexual. There is a vast difference between girl time and boy time. (For purposes of completeness, it might also be noted that there is a difference between your time and my time, between kid time and adult time, and between work time and vacation time. But all of that is for another time and place.)

For example, when a guy says "I'll call you soon," he means when I get around to it, if I remember, when I've straightened out my love life, when I get my finances in order, once the baseball season has ended, or never.

To a woman, "soon" means within the next twenty-four hours at most, but preferably when you get home since you're so smitten with me you probably are going to be awake all night anyway.

As you might guess, this time differential can create lots of problems. To begin with, our female heroine is sitting all dewy-eyed by the telephone, has hung up on her mother twice, has told her girlfriends (in whom she has confided the breathless details of her newest and by far most promising romance) to keep the line clear for his call, and has instructed her secretary to keep everybody but the boss off the line. She has arranged to have the phone monitored around the clock and for food to be delivered. Her laundry is piling up, since risking a missed phone call is worse than having to wear slightly mussed garments to work. The apartment will not benefit from the vigil, since the vacuum cleaner might drown out the phone ring. As the hours stretch into days and the days into weeks, she is no longer dewy-eyed but furious, and she feels that one more time she has been misled, betrayed, and generally played for a sucker.

This state of mind does not bode well for any male who finally gets around to calling, having returned from a business trip, cleared some time on his calendar, finished a crucial project, or dumped some part of a relationship that was going nowhere and should have ended months ago. He now has his courage up, has planned a date or at least a phone conversation, and he's met with (1) stony silence; (2) a blank when he mentions his first name; (3) sarcastic remarks about his stopped watch or the number of funerals he must have been attending to prevent his calling or the trauma of his having been taken hostage in a part of the world so remote as to have been untouched by the phone company.

What's wrong with this picture? Basically, the difference between girl time and boy time. In general, women seem to be in more of a hurry about relationships and especially about commitment. So whenever time is discussed in the abstract—"We'll get engaged soon," or "We'll meet your parents soon"—warning bells should go off in both your heads; beware the word "soon."

THE RESOLUTION

Guys, when you say you're going to call, never use the word "soon" and never say you're going to call unless you think there is at least a 75 percent chance you might actually do so in the next week. Then it's easy. If you're not sure when you're going to call, say you'll try to get back to her in the next week. If you're going to be out of town, say so. If you're involved in a relationship, you can either admit that or just say you're kind of tied up for the next month or so, but would like to call after the holidays or when you're a little older and wiser. Just don't say "soon."

Gals, if he says, "I'll call you soon," you can say, "I'm going to be in and out for the next couple of days—why don't you give me your number and I'll call you in the next week." It's also okay to say, "What does 'soon' mean to you?"—but he may justifiably feel that you're being a little overeager. It's also okay to say, "I'm sure you're not one of those guys who would say you're going to call and then not call. It's so silly to mislead people that way."

If it seems as though we're talking simple courtesy, you're right, but we're also talking about using the same word to mean significantly different things. If somehow the word "soon" has passed your lips, fellows, realize the sooner the better. The longer you take to get in touch, the more vulnerable and uncomfortable she's likely to be, and the more likely she's going to feel the need to protect herself at your expense. First, she will try to figure out what she did wrong and blame herself. Then she will begin to decide that you're a rat or a coward or a heartbreaker or some awful combination of the three. By the time you get around to calling . . . well, you get the point.

Two final points, guys. If you really do intend to call her back, you'd be amazed at the benefits you'll reap from calling sooner rather than later. The next day will win you brownie points you wouldn't believe. On an even more important, global level, male/female interaction would immeasurably improve if men could stop viewing time as something you can stretch, withhold, and waste.

Women, cut him some slack. Don't be so passive; it's perfectly good form to ask for clarification if you're not clear about what he means.

Both of you may want to do something as simple as defining what you each mean by the word "soon." You may discover that your meanings differ significantly, but at least you'll be aware of the problem and can decide how to compromise. It may not even be a matter of one of you slowing down and the other speeding up but more a matter of understanding what each of you means initially. Then you can compromise.

One final word about time. Adults value one another's time. If you're always late, you need to clean up your act or plan better. Wasting someone's time is an act of disrespect and condescension. You wouldn't keep your boss waiting—you might keep your subordinate waiting. So unless you want to be constantly battling power issues in your relationship, get in the habit of valuing each other's time. If there are power issues to be resolved, deal with them head on, don't act them out.

Time perceptions are complicated enough for physicists; for lovers, time can truly be a black hole in an ever-expanding universe. Time is the most valuable thing on the planet; it's the only thing we can never get more of. Once it's gone, so are we. Treat it accordingly.

Female Overtures

♥

THE GAME

She's an Eighties woman. She sees him jogging several days in a row, smiles when he asks how's it going. At the drinking fountain in the park where they're both getting some water, they chat. She says maybe it would be fun to see each other dressed, asks him where he works, and gives him a call at work the next day. He sounds surprised, but delighted to hear from her, and they make a date for drinks for the following week. Drinks becomes dinner. They go back to her apartment for a nightcap. He makes a pass. She says slow down. He intensifies his efforts. She says stop. He doesn't. She slugs him. He calls her a tease and a frigid bitch and leaves. She decides all men are only after one thing.

THE BLAME

HE figures that she gets her jollies setting men up, luring them to her apartment, and then shutting down. He figures she hates all men and just enjoys getting them hot and bothered so they look and feel foolish. He figures she's probably a little on the lesbian side anyway. Usually he can spot the type, but she seemed sweeter and softer. He probably should have just gone ahead and raped her—it's what she probably wanted anyhow.

SHE is convinced that her mother was right. Men really are after sex and sex alone. Her taking a more active role seemed only to bring out his chauvinism. She can't believe she was so stupid as to trust him enough to let him up to her apartment. He seemed nice and wholesome, but then he practically raped her.

THE EXPLANATION

As traditional roles change, both men and women are left in a confusing no-man's land where the signals are often misunderstood. Her assertiveness combined with her willingness in allowing herself to be more or less picked up in the park and then taking the initiative about the first date all played into his fantasy and/or expectation that she was most likely going to be more sexually accessible than most women. To a lot of men, "liberated" means "sexually liberated" (read: hot to trot, available, adventurous, aggressive, and hopefully even mildly promiscuous). Whether it's true or not, a portion of the power in sexual relationships has been shifted. Some men are cowed by this lessening of control, while others are excited by the idea of being sexually (not socially, just sexually) passive, to be done to rather than doing.

Unfortunately, all of her cues fed into his fantasy and expectations, from making the overtures, to asking him out, to paying for dinner, to inviting him up for a drink. He figured she was looking for the same thing he would have been looking for if he was taking the initiative; and so the combination of his arousal and his willingness to help her out resulted in his reasserting his characteristic male role. By the time he figured out that sex wasn't really what she had on her mind, it was too late. His face and his penis both had to be saved, so he pushed for what seemed to him a reasonable conclusion.

However, regardless of what she did or didn't do to excite him, *anything after the word "no" is rape,* and in spite of a recent survey suggesting that fifth-graders think it is okay to expect sex if you've spent ten dollars or more on another person, bodies are sovereign and *everybody* has the right to say no at any time.

She failed to understand that when something is taken away, something is expected in exchange. While she enjoys having the initiative and being a bit more in control, to him that aggressiveness allowed for and was consistent with sexual aggressiveness as well. It may be that her unfamiliarity with the role of social aggressor made her a bit awkward and caused her to revert to a behavior more flirtatious than usual. Everything was probably okay until she invited him up for a nightcap. Had the roles been reversed and she had accepted his offer it would have meant tacit acceptance of his making a pass at her. It's likely she never would have consented to visiting his apartment after only one date. On that basis alone, it is then unwise to invite him up. While it's her turf and her evening, it is impossible to overturn centuries of conditioning in one evening. This isn't to justify his unwillingness to hear her when she says no but to suggest that putting oneself in a sexually ambiguous situation with a stranger is dangerous. Whether it's fair or not, once behavior leaves the expected or traditional realms, unspoken expectations are dangerous.

THE RESOLUTION

This unfortunate scenario doesn't suggest that women have to return to acting like shrinking violets, nor that men have to resume the tiresome burden of always taking the social and sexual initiative, but it does suggest that changing the rules takes some care and more than the usual talking out loud. If you're changing the rules of a card game, it's wise to play a few hands open, so everybody can see everybody else's cards until the rules are clear to all the players.

Most men still harbor the fantasy that there is some sexy creature out there who is willing to be a hybrid of Mother Earth, courtesan, protector, and bimbo. If a woman takes over some of those roles it may conjure up fantasies of the rest. This doesn't mean she has to fulfill them, but her being aware of his expectations can save a lot of wear and tear on couches, tear ducts, stomach linings, and date books.

It's never okay for either sex to go beyond *no* under any circumstances. Not only must bodies be sovereign, but responsibility must be taken for saying what we mean and meaning what we say. Each of us must be able to say "yes" as well as "no" as well as "maybe," and if "no" doesn't mean anything then neither does "yes."

Changing role behavior offers great possibility for misunderstanding, frustration, and hurt feelings, but also for fun, stimulation, empathy, insight, compassion, courage, and education. The outcome depends primarily on communication, openness, and a willingness to look a little silly and awkward from time to time.

Will Sex Ruin the Friendship?

THE GAME

They have been best friends forever, confiding the intimate details of life to each other in often hushed tones, counting on each other to supply insight and humor, an occasional shoulder to cry on, and reassurance when things got dicey. Then one day, the light was just right and they realized, "Me Tarzan, you Jane," and it was a whole new game, or rather the same old game only now they wanted to play it together. The question for both of them was, would sex ruin a perfectly good friendship?

THE BLAME

Blame wasn't really an issue yet, but what both of them feared, she more than he.

SHE had seen it happen time and time again. When sex came into the picture, she became clingy, he became distant, and the movie *Tootsie* said it all. Once friends hop into the sack, he treats her like any other conquest, forgets to call, cheats, stops treating her like a special friend. It almost makes you believe in the Sicilian view of the universe. No such thing as friendship between males and females, just sex looking for a place to happen. She values him for what they have now.

HE finds her wonderfully attractive. She makes him feel better about himself for being able to love her mind well before noticing that she's got a great body. As far as he's concerned, it's the relationship of his dreams: somebody he likes and trusts and respects and has gotten to know *before* they do the dirty. He understands her reservations, but figures it can only get better.

THE EXPLANATION

SHE is more cautious, because she feels that men have more power in a relationship once a woman has said yes. She doesn't know many men who sit around waiting for the phone to ring. It's not only an issue of power, but as things are she can call him without feeling embarrassed or wondering if he's with another woman. If he is, she'll hear all about it and won't have to feel the least bit jealous or competitive. She understands the nature of friendship better than he does, since she's been practicing it longer, has more friends, and spends more time thinking and talking about the whole issue. Most men she knows either have no really close intimate friends or have a woman for a best friend. She loves him dearly, but is just not sure he understands what both of them would be risking. She really values the friendship greatly and is therefore more reluctant to jeopardize it.

HE is probably more comfortable with sex, since he has been at it longer, is more comfortable with his own sexuality, and is used to being in control at least after she's said yes. It's not that he's on a power trip, it's just that he's curious and enticed and available right now. He figures the worst that could happen is that the sex wouldn't work out and they could go back to being just friends. He doesn't understand that to her, friend is probably higher on the list than lover. Lovers come and go, but her friends sustain her.

She is more reluctant going in, but if she resorts to what he sees as the common pattern of female dependence and passivity once they've had sex, her fears that he will consider her like all his other women may very well be realized. Her appeal may be of the unknown, and once she's known, literally, figuratively, and biblically, some of her appeal to him and her emotional independence from him may diminish. Because she better understands both the role of friendship and female emotional investment in sexual relationships, she is more reluctant to become sexually involved.

If they should decide to "do it," she may very well become more comfortable in the relationship, since she knows him and trusts him, and he may become less comfortable, since he has lost a confidante (she most likely has several) and gained a more possessive bed partner and may be conflicted by that old male bugaboo intimacy and the problems of feeling drawn to a strong woman. (Friendship is based on more equality than most sexual relationships are, if only because of societal convention and a millennium of conditioning.)

THE RESOLUTION

This relationship has much to offer both parties. The pitfalls are at least theoretically equal for both. As are the rewards. Each needs to be completely honest with self and the other about expectations, secret fantasies, fears, drawbacks, penalties, and rewards.

If they do decide to consummate the relationship and it works out (whatever that means), they may indeed have the basis for a lasting, extraordinary relationship. They may have that basis even without the sex, but only if both remain strong enough in the security of the friendship to remain their best, strongest, truest selves and not resort to the way they behave with other members of the opposite sex with whom they become romantically involved. It can be a rich learning experience for both. Her risks have to do mostly with passivity and dependency. His have to do with intimacy and control. If each is aware going in and careful once involved, the friendship doesn't have to be at risk. If the new level of involvement works for neither, friendship can probably be resumed after an interval when each has become reinvolved with other people. If it works out, they're home free and blessed. There can be trouble if one person is satisfied and the other dissatisfied, but if both are honest and willing to be gentle as well as to let the healing time elapse, friendship can probably be resumed eventually.

It is the ultimate fantasy for both men and women. Women are just more aware of the intricacies of friendship and therefore more reluctant initially. Men often feel trapped and guilty afterward. On the other hand, life is daring risk or it's nothing at all. Just be aware and careful of the other's feelings and your own expectations.

Old Flames

♥

THE GAME

They have just begun dating and are cozily curled up in front of the fireplace, sipping wine, cuddling, and reminiscing about their respective high school experiences. He begins to describe in exquisite detail his first real girlfriend. She listens with a bemused smile that gets increasingly more strained as he continues to wax eloquent about her body, her ability to kiss, her legs, her cute little . . .

At this point, she has had enough; she wraps herself in the blanket, storms off to the bathroom, and locks herself in. He can't figure out what has happened.

THE BLAME

HE feels that she is jealous and immature. After all, this took place years ago and he's quite clearly crazy about her. She is so moody and unpredictable. Maybe she's just about to get her period.

SHE thinks that he's a callous lout. He knows she's trying very hard to lose those extra couple of pounds, and comparing her to this fantasy of eighteen-year-old perfection is mean and petty and just one more example of his insensitivity.

THE EXPLANATION

Without really being conscious of the fact, many men talk about former conquests as a way of turning on their current partner. Even when the discussion isn't blatantly sexual, a man often feels that providing evidence that other women have found him attractive will make any woman appreciate him more. Men have been turning each other on in the locker room for years with just such stories; it's a way of showing off, feeling proud without exactly bragging, and one good story always seems to elicit another. He may be hoping that if he shares, she'll share, and it might be fun to hear about her past. Additionally, he may feel that she will be flattered that he is with her given his options. With all of these seemingly good reasons to talk sexy, it's not surprising that somehow it occurs to very few men unless some wise former girlfriend clues them in, that talking about past conquests is not only *not* sexy, but tacky, hurtful, and often humiliating.

A woman is much less likely to share such information, not necessarily because her intelligence is superior or her manners better, but more likely because many women, even today, are still trying to appear to be, if not vestal virgins, at least not too far from innocence. Once married or in a committed relationship, men tend to keep old liaisons quiet (perhaps because mentioning them can focus undue suspicions on new ones), while women tend to be quite willing to invite a former beau over for supper to rattle a husband's complacent assumption that he is and has always been the only man in her life.

THE RESOLUTION

Instead of storming off and being hurt and angry, she might tactfully inquire why he is telling her all of this. To his "Gee, I just thought you wanted to know everything about me," she might respond that knowing about the important people in your life is interesting and important, but all of the details are a bit overwhelming, so maybe broad, general outlines are best and she can ask questions on a need-to-know basis. Then, *resist the temptation to ask questions*. What's done is done, and if it's not done, then he should tell you that it's not. If she continues to make a federal case out of any woman in his past, he will have (1) a perfect alibi to withhold any information about any woman at any time on the grounds that "when I told you about women I hadn't seen for twenty years, you went crazy, so why should I mention that I drove my boss's wife home from shopping on Friday"; (2) a reason to stop telling her *anything* about anything; (3) a perception of her as an insecure, paranoid harpy.

Men, there are other less dangerous ways of making sure that she recognizes that you need to be appreciated for the wonderful, desirable, manly creature that you are. Bragging about past conquests is tricky in the locker room and downright suicidal in the bedroom.

Telling All

THE GAME

They have known each other for four weeks. They enjoy each other's company, they laugh a lot together. They've been to bed, and it seems that things are progressing favorably. One evening they have gone to bed early and are both enjoying the afterglow of sex, and one or the other suggests that they "tell all." She says, "You first." So he begins to describe his "parade of women." She feels as if someone had thrown a glass of ice water at her. He is seemingly oblivious to her fury, which makes her angrier. She decides to retaliate by going into graphic detail about her previous lovers. Somehow the mood is broken.

THE BLAME

SHE thinks he is an insensitive clod for the way he talks about the other women he has been with. She is not so naïve as to assume that she's the first woman in his life, but his combination of macho bragging and callous dismissal of all those others instantly puts her on guard. She sure doesn't want to be one more tuba in his parade.

Heretofore, she'd been perfectly content with their lovemaking. He seemed interested and involved and made her feel special, and now to find out that in another few months, she'll just be a decimal point in his Dewey Decimal System makes her feel cheap and used.

HE feels diminished and jealous and competitive. While the details of her previous encounters were sort of sexy and fun to hear about, he is now convinced that he simply doesn't measure up to her previous lovers (yes, in *that* department, too) and that she is constantly comparing him to all her previous lovers.

He is used to bragging to the guys in somewhat abstract terms about his exploits, and since he really didn't name any names, he has done the gentlemanly thing by protecting any particular woman's reputation. He just wanted her to think that he's sexually experienced, popular, and cool. If she is conscious of his other women, she won't be angry or surprised if one pops up or he confuses names, but mostly, he just wants her to know that he's no nerd when it comes to sex and he can fully appreciate her, since she's not his first woman.

And about her confessions. He just can't get it out of his mind that she not only isn't a virgin, but is experienced enough to know that he's not all that proficient in the sexual department. He's always been a little insecure about the size of his penis. He's lucky if he's not impotent the next time they try and make love.

THE EXPLANATION

Men are used to talking with each other about their exploits (see previous chapter) and since many are unsure about what to talk to women about, it may be that they figure they may as well try the same ploy. After all, it always kept their buddies interested and enhanced their status. If men thought about it, they very likely wouldn't share the information, especially in such an offhand fashion (which they assume is what makes it all okay to begin with). But intimacy, especially conversational intimacy, is a new experience for a lot of men, so they do what they've done before, talk about "guy stuff." Since they already know baseball scores and work won't cut it, they might try a conversation about past experience, which, especially if they don't think it through, may very well lead them astray. Men also really do worry about penis size, even though most women find size nearly irrelevant. Years of trying to measure up, literally and figuratively, seem to have left their mark on most men, no matter how seemingly secure, hence the trap in talking about past exploits.

Women have less of an excuse for talking about past liaisons. Most women are not all that comfortable being viewed as sexual Olympic contenders. Her blunder in presenting herself as fairly experienced is most likely due to a combination of anger, a wish to get even and show that she too has been loved, and a wish to be honest and have him know and love and accept the "real" her. She may also feel that it's a compliment to him that she values him as a lover even though she isn't completely inexperienced.

THE RESOLUTION

When it comes to sex, while neither party needs to maintain the stance of virginity unless one actually happens to be a virgin, the less said about previous encounters of the close kind the better. Nobody is interested in hearing about the terrific dinner you had with somebody else at another restaurant while you're dining with your current companion. Discussion of past sexual sorties is about as appropriate and appetizing. Don't do it. You don't have to lie, but good sex has to do with communication and closeness in the here and now, *not* the then and there. Between honesty and duplicity lies silence. When it comes to past lovers, silence is golden and safe. If absolutely unavoidable, a quiet "so-and-so was then, you're now; the past is over, and I prefer to live the present and be with you" should suffice. Amen.

This truly is one of those times to stonewall. A discussion of past sexual exploits does neither partner any good. If there have been problems in the past, they are probably best resolved with a competent professional (most often by talking about them and rethinking, not reenacting, the problems, so they can be sorted through). Keeping score isn't sexy, polite, or wise. Trust me on this one, regardless of the temptations of the moment.

The Restaurant

THE GAME

They have gone to her favorite restaurant. In the past, he has picked the restaurants, but she doesn't want to appear passive and thought he might enjoy a brief foray into her world. The captain who usually greets her isn't around, but they have been seated and are ready to order. Their waitress barely speaks English, and he almost immediately begins to berate her when she fails to adequately answer his questions. She smiles weakly and tries to smooth things over with both him and the waitress. Another waitress is summoned who is openly rude. The manager finally is called over. In the interim, he says to prepare to leave. The manager rather ineffectually says these things happen. He is furious, she is uncomfortable. What started out as a pleasant experiment has now become unpleasant and tense. Both hurriedly finish their meal and leave with a bad taste in their mouths that has very little to do with the food.

THE BLAME

HE feels with some justification that she didn't really support him against the waitresses. He was willing to try her restaurant and was even somewhat pleased by her offering to make a decision and plan some of their time together rather than just saying, "I'd like to do whatever you want, dear." While the waitresses' rudeness to him is not directly her fault, her loyalty to him was slight if not nonexistent.

SHE wishes she had never suggested the whole stupid thing. She just thought it might be fun for him if he didn't have to make all the decisions. He could have been a little calmer with the waitress, and she actually wouldn't have minded leaving, but once he decided to stay, he could have relaxed a bit and been a good sport about the whole thing. As it is, the evening was a disaster, she's not sure she'll ever suggest another restaurant, and she's afraid she won't feel comfortable returning to the place that used to be her favorite.

THE EXPLANATION

This is one of those painful situations in which nobody is really to blame, but the explicit and the implicit have ganged up on both him and her to contribute to a real mess. First, both were trying to break out of preexisting rules about how men and women act on dates, with men doing manly things like making decisions and reservations and using their credit cards. In taking responsibility for the evening, she was entering, if not uncharted territory, at least an area of unclear rules and uncertain expectations—certainly reason for anxiety. She was feeling proud of herself, but a little uncomfortable. He was flattered and pleased, but also uncomfortable, not in control. The incompetent first waitress and rude second one were sent by some whimsical, capricious spirit to test their commitment to true equality. She wasn't in the traditional position of deference and even the waitresses whose job it is to serve him were unwilling to defer. She wanted everything to be perfect to show that she was a grown-up, equal partner. Both of them are still in the early days of a relationship, when mistakes loom large because of so little shared history.

And then there's the really big item. Men have been taught since the cradle to stand up and fight for their rights. Women, by and large, have been taught to make nice. Making a fuss, sending food back, asking for special service, losing one's temper—such behavior is expected only of somebody who is used to paying the bills and hence is in control in a service situation. And in this society, that means the man.

Most women feel at least some sympathy with a woman who is serving food, since it is a role with which they can readily identify, and they don't like the idea of making a fuss. Aggressiveness is by and large considered unfeminine. In this case, it's not even that she feels he is wrong, just that she doesn't see the point. To him, it's an important point, a matter of face, status, and, of course power. He was already a bit off balance, and the inability of one waitress and the unwillingness of the other to grant his wishes were bound to infuriate him. She would have calmed him down only by showing the most extreme subservience to compensate. Even then, it would probably not work.

THE RESOLUTION

HE probably should have admitted that while he likes her willingness to take charge occasionally, it's still a little new to him and it makes him a bit uncomfortable.

SHE might do well to admit exactly the same thing. She might also discuss her reluctance to make a fuss in public. She got caught by her unwillingness to take a stand. By staying in the middle, she allowed both sides to misbehave. She could have (1) supported his confrontation, (2) asked him to cut it out, (3) asked him if he wanted to stay or go rather than enduring his sulks.

There is something wonderful and exciting for each in venturing into new territories that have previously been the exclusive province of the other. But the one whose territory is being invaded is often going to feel some need, conscious or not, to reassert his or her former role. This shouldn't prevent either partner from making such explorations, but both are advised to proceed with a certain amount of care and be aware of the other's awkwardness. That way glitches can be handled rather than being sources of conflict or deterrents to further trips to the "other" side.

Men have been bred for aggressive behavior, and women feel some fundamental need to smooth over and make nice. If we admit this difference rather than try to ignore it, we might all learn lots about each other, not to mention ourselves. For the short term, however, we can't expect to overturn thousands of years of conditioning and social expectation either easily or overnight. Hang in there, everybody—we're all in this together.

Sex and Intimacy

♥

THE GAME

It's been a great evening of wining and dining. They have been holding hands and gazing into each other's eyes and giggling and having a generally terrific time. He can hardly wait to get her home to fulfill the promise of the evening. He's feeling romantic and sexy, and even though they haven't known each other long, she may be the one. They neck in the cab on the way home. He can hardly believe it when she skips out of the cab, throwing him a kiss, and disappears behind her front door. He feels he's been had, robbed, and he wouldn't call that female con artist again if she were the last woman on the face of the earth. And he was thinking seriously about her.

THE BLAME

SHE is no dummy, and when she doesn't hear from him, she figures he's just one more guy who thinks that for the price of dinner and drinks, he's assured of scoring. Her mother was right, and for all his manners, flowers, sweetness, he's interested in only one thing. As far as she's concerned, it's love me, love my mind.

54

HE thinks that she's a tease and that the whole thing has been a setup—she wanted to see how hot and bothered she could get him and then play Ice Goddess Who's Above All This Animal Stuff.

THE EXPLANATION

If all of the differences between men and women could be boiled down to one issue, it would be the difference between sex and intimacy. It has long been held that men trade intimacy for sex and women trade sex for intimacy, but it may be far worse than that; it may be that both men and women confuse the two.

HE feels that by coming on to a woman, he is demonstrating his need for intimacy and willingness to be intimate. He is thus confused when he pays a woman a compliment by referring to a particularly enticing part of her anatomy and she reacts by becoming haughty, huffy, and hostile. She says she wants to know what he's thinking, but apparently if he's thinking about sex, she doesn't want to know. He concludes that women are squeamish about sex and really *want* to be lied to and have everything wrapped up pretty, even though they know deep down what's going on. As the song says, it's okay to make promises, since they don't expect you to keep them anyway. He knows women are vulnerable romantics, which is why he's careful not to mislead them. He knows better than to spend the night— sex is one thing, intimacy quite something else. Intimacy is about feeling close to a woman, and feeling close to his mom was scary because he had to be a man. Intimacy too soon can feel suffocating. It's always a good idea to leave some space, an escape hatch, so he doesn't feel overwhelmed.

SHE has been schooled since the cradle to be an intimacy junkie. As far as she's concerned, it's what love is all about. Sex is okay, once she can trust the guy and knows he really likes her. It's not that she's trying to be the Ice Goddess, it's just that sex is something sacred. After all, it's *inside* her body, and she is her body. Sex makes her feel vulnerable. She's willing to use it occasionally to settle a fight or as a pacifier. But while she knows it's okay to like sex, being the initiator or taking too active a role may make him think she's really experienced or that she's a whore, and even if he doesn't think so, her mom sure would. The distinction between Ice Goddess and Nice Girl isn't easy for her to draw.

THE RESOLUTION

Strong emotions make both him and her feel vulnerable, and when we feel vulnerable, we want to be taken care of. For women, being taken care of means being nurtured. Such nurturing originally came from Mom or Dad and was all about intimacy. For men, being taken care of may mean the same thing, but boys aren't usually encouraged to be particularly intimate with their Dads, and being too intimate with Mom makes you a mama's boy. So the more emotional a man feels, the more terrifying his feelings may be, at least initially. Given this dilemma, both he and she have to evolve different ways of responding to feelings of vulnerability, since asking to be taken care of won't work for either in the long run.

The only way to evolve these new roles is to be aware of the need and the tendency to express feelings of vulnerability in old, childlike ways rather than to talk about them.

For example, instead of setting herself up as the Nice Girl who won't go to bed with a man until he tells her he loves her, thereby encouraging him to lie in order to satisfy his sexual needs, she might try to convince him that she too is interested in a sexual relationship and that if he will give her a little time she will actually help him seduce her. Thus an adversarial relationship is turned into a cooperative one. She might also explain, "I get more involved once I've gone to bed with a man, and I don't want to make unreasonable demands or fall madly in love with you or be unrealistic in my expectations."

If he's terrified of intimacy he is likely to skedaddle, and if he's not you've offered a timetable and a scenario that leaves both of you some maneuverability. If bed it is to be, it may be sooner than the Ice Goddess would have permitted and later than his arousal would have dictated, but early enough to convince him that she's flesh and blood and passionate and real and late enough to convince her that he truly is interested in all parts of her, not just those that are covered by a bathing suit.

The Marriage Con

THE GAME

They have been introduced by a mutual friend who has told each of them they were made for each other. After the usual preliminaries, they set about the process of getting to know each other by exchanging information— birthplace, birthdate, family origin, occupation. Her birthday is a month away and when she tells him this she coyly inquires what he plans to get her for the occasion. He calmly replies, "An engagement ring." Being a sophisticated end-of-the-century woman, she responds by asking whether she should call the caterer or will he. Equally cool, he responds that he has a guy he usually uses. For a first date, things seem to be moving rapidly. They neck on the sidewalk in front of her apartment, talk on the phone until four in the morning three nights running. He then disappears off the face of the earth.

THE BLAME

HE has done nothing more than be cute. He found out years ago that appearing to be incredibly interested on the first date is a much more effective technique than being blasé. It costs him nothing, and often as not it results in his being able to bed a woman sooner rather than later. He can't imagine that she took him seriously, and while it's all been fun, it's now back to life as usual.

SHE realizes that on some level he is kidding but finds it easy and comfortable and exciting to believe that finally here is a man who knows what he wants and isn't afraid to admit it as well as go for it. She's tired of all the cautious wimps she has dated in the past who wait months to call and even then make certain that she understands that she is simply one of many and will have to wait her turn. Her head knows it's all too good to be true, but her heart has been sucked in by the speed and the romance and his certainty. When he fails to call after the first week, she feels either that she has done something terribly wrong or that he is a total heel who only wanted a trophy for his ego room.

THE EXPLANATION

Both men and women have believed for so long that women are all predators bent on taking away a man's freedom and conning him into marriage that women now pretend they don't want to get married and men pretend they do. Reality for both is usually somewhere in between, but closer to the historical stereotype than either is comfortable admitting.

He has found out that the quickest way to a woman's bed is via her willingness to believe that he is committed to her, and what more dramatic statement of commitment is there than offering marriage on the first date?

She is so used to pretending she is modern and liberated that she appears to be nonchalant and dismissive about the big M. She figures she can snare him by appearing to be willing to forgo a commitment.

His technique will be effective only if she secretly desires what he is offering and is therefore willing to believe his preposterous stance. Obviously he's right—score one for him.

His disappearing act may be the result of his feeling that he has moved too fast, or that she really is worth courting but he's already so far ahead of himself that he has no second act. Or it may be that he's a complete heel who is in fact taking advantage of his insight and of her. Or maybe what started as a joke has gotten out of hand and he has to get back to normal life and doesn't know how to explain.

We tend to believe in love at first sight, because it combines two of the qualities we hold most dear: romance and efficiency. It's the McDonald's approach to love, instant and hot and our way. It's a trap for everyone, since it bypasses the time it takes to establish a firm, realistic basis for a relationship and replaces it with mutual, dovetailing fantasies of what each person needs and wants as opposed to what each is. The process of discovery takes time. Love at first sight is lust with potential—and it usually includes the potential for disaster unless the process is slowed.

THE RESOLUTION

He and she are both playing games—time-honored but destructive games about how men and women act. He is busily playing the swashbuckling pursuer while she is playing the shy virgin. If each had been a bit more honest the whole situation could have been avoided. For example, he could decide that proposing marriage on a first date might be very effective to the short-term objective of melting her defenses, but is a very expensive technique in the long run in terms of trust. She could realize that he had just pushed her most magic and secret of all buttons and told him so, which would have either stopped him dead in his tracks, allowed him the opportunity to turn the whole thing into a joke, or scared the willies out of him—any of which would have wrought less havoc than their rather confused *pas de deux*.

She might have been alerted to his ambivalence by his willingness to have long phone conversations without even a mention of getting together. Again, his understanding of what women really want—undemanding attention—allows him to appear more interested than he really is. Her passivity allows him to spin his web of fantasy. His technique depends on her fear of admitting her true wishes; he can use them to entwine her.

If they could figure out what each of them wants from the other and admit it to themselves as well as to each other, they'd be more likely to ask for what they want, increase the probability of getting it as well as be less likely to hurt or be hurt.

Doing Too Much

♥

THE GAME

They met on a plane, spent twelve hours chatting each other up, exchanged business cards, and promised to go out for dinner should either be in the same city at the same time. Both returned home aware of the difficulties of long-distance romances, but still, there did seem to be that spark.

He has called every night since they met, sent her dozens of cute cards, and flowers on the weekly anniversary of their first date, talked about how many kids they should have and how she would feel about living in Brazil for a couple of years. They have planned to go away together for ten days at Christmas. The week before Christmas, he sends her a telegram saying his business is in trouble, and she never hears from him again.

THE BLAME

SHE feels he played her for a fool, and the name of the game was seduction, not involvement. While she doesn't doubt that his business is suffering, she's not sure why she has to suffer as well. She feels bereft and humiliated, especially since she told her friends that she'd finally met Señor Right.

HE wants her to understand that business comes first and that it's certainly not his fault that things got messed up—but he's afraid she won't understand. He intends to make things right as quickly as possible, and feels that he is more to be pitied than despised. After all, it's not really his fault that his business is floundering, and he feels panicky about wasting valuable time mollifying her. Besides, he's embarrassed as well as disappointed.

THE EXPLANATION

SHE may be right. If he is a man who is more interested in the challenge than the consummation, she has given him what he wants by allowing herself to be swept off her feet. The more she trusts him, the more trustworthy she expects him to be, which is exactly backward. If he is the type to be easily overwhelmed, she is playing directly into his hands by expecting a lot and perhaps offering too much in return. She has put all of her emotional eggs in his basket, admittedly with his encouragement. He obviously has not put all his emotional eggs in her basket; assuming his business problems are legitimate, lots of his eggs are rolling around in his commercial carrier.

HE is involved in his business. He feels guilty for letting her down and believes that in order to redeem himself, he must have everything in perfect shape. He is embarrassed. As time goes on, it becomes harder and harder to face her, although he never meant to let things drop completely. He feels horrible about himself and assumes that she must feel that way about him too. He's assuming that she's written him off as the loser he feels himself to be. It would never occur to him that she might still be willing to be involved with him.

THE RESOLUTION

The underlying, unacknowledged issue for both of them is power and control. In his sweeping her off her feet, he controls the interaction aggressively, she passively, until she capitulates and then he is in complete control. She attempts to control the relationship by remaining aloof for as long as possible, and then in her capitulation, she attempts to control him by demanding that he respond in kind, literally killing with kindness. The unspoken contract is: okay, I'm doing it your way, because you wanted it, but now you owe me, buster. These contracts are as old as time and are difficult to acknowledge and unravel. It is only when both parties are willing to be honest and straightforward about what they want that pain can be avoided. But even then it's hard to avoid it entirely, since both parties have to *know* what they want, both consciously and unconsciously. And he (or she) who cares least controls the relationship, which is what a lot of posturing between men and women is all about to begin with.

Caring for another person increases one's vulnerability, which makes it especially important to go slowly, to attempt to be honest, and to understand that men and women feel and show vulnerability in different ways. Men need to find the courage to be involved rather than just in control, and women need to be more disciplined and to resist the temptation to be swept away, abandoning friends, small animals, responsibilities, and reason to the L word. If both parties are willing to lower expectations, modify behavior, and accept the discomfort of vulnerability, then claustrophobia and bullying can give way to mild discomfort and uncertainty and a relationship may have time to grow.

Children

♥

THE GAME

On their third date, he asks her how she feels about kids in general, having them in particular, and how many how soon. He asks whether she believes in working mothers, in Pampers or cloth diapers. He asks whether pacifiers really cause secure kids or wealthy orthodontists.

She is enchanted with his sincerity, his humanity, and she feels at last she has found a new-age male. Even though the relationship is barely off the ground, she is willing to overlook a lot, since she feels she has at last found an unselfish man who is committed to her and to settling down. When she tells her best friend Betsy, Betsy says, "run, don't walk—this guy is a real loser. He's manipulating you." Betsy always knows best—so now, what's a girl to do?

THE BLAME

HE is getting a bit ahead of himself. Although she may feel in retrospect that he has used this ploy as seduction, that is not actually his intent. He feels that he is being honest and up front about wanting to have a child and is busily congratulating himself on the fact that he is a cut above the rest of the male population in being truly unselfish and ready to commit.

SHE agrees with Betsy that he is using the ploy to get her into bed; that for him babies are just another word for having sex and he probably can't shake his puritan upbringing and enjoy sex for its own sake without offering her not only a wedding ring but a nursery simultaneously.

THE EXPLANATION

Both he and she have missed the point. All of a sudden it has become fashionable for men of certain age to try to prove that they are not the shallow, selfish, hedonistic creatures they have feared they might be by claiming that a baby would make their lives complete and that they are capable of relating in a kind, caring manner to another human being. The only troubles are that (1) a baby is the world's easiest creature to relate to; (2) babies have an annoying habit of growing into children who demand more than an occasional hug; and (3) women often resent being thought of as incubators.

Admittedly, things between the sexes have gotten a bit hostile over the last several years partly as a result of our attempts to figure out just what everybody wants and needs to feel happy and content and cherished and loved. But deciding that a good way to satisfy such wants and needs is via a third, helpless creature is a mistake for all concerned, including the baby.

Americans already devote themselves to relationships

that are child-centered to the neglect of both adult members. Hence the large number of neurotic children and marriages that fall apart once the children have left. Children need to know they can be loved when they are adults, and the best way to understand the concept is by example. If the best thing a child can be is a child, there is no inherent motivation for him to move toward independence and adulthood, let alone marriage and parenting.

THE RESOLUTION

Both men and women need to understand that children are a time-consuming, resource-gobbling, temporary item in a relationship. They demand much and offer little. If either partner feels the need to base self-worth on the role of parent, either or both should probably think in terms of nursery-school teacher, pediatrician, baby-sitter, loving aunt or uncle, or Mr. Rogers. Feeling that loving a child is the road to humanity or the cure for lagging self-esteem is unrealistic and unfair to an adult partner or a child victim.

Friends: The Guys

♥

THE GAME

They've been seeing each other for three months. He gets a call from his old friend Joe to go out Friday night and party down. She views Friday night as their special night and decides that the perfect compromise is for them to double-date with Joe and his girlfriend, if he has one, or she is willing to fix Joe up with one of her friends. Her love absolutely refuses. She is shattered and concludes that he cares more about his stupid friend than about her and their relationship.

THE BLAME

HE feels that they spend lots of time together and his friends have been taking a backseat. He needs a breather and tells himself that if she doesn't trust him, he's had just about enough. He has no intention of misbehaving while out with his friend, but if she's going to treat him this way, he just might consider getting rowdy.

SHE is really secretly hurt that he hasn't seen fit to introduce her to any of his friends, and when she questions him about it, he says they're kind of rough and are only interested in chasing girls anyway, and she would have nothing in common with them. She had viewed the call from his friend as the perfect opportunity to kill two birds with one stone; meet some of his friends and prove that she could fit in. She's now convinced that either he's ashamed of her or he's planning to cheat on her.

THE EXPLANATION

Men and women have different needs for intimacy and different definitions of "friend." In this instance, the two definitions came crashing into each other. She is an intimacy junkie and wants to spend all of her free time with him. She confides all of her really important secrets to her friends on the phone and has happily introduced him to her friends after the second date. She is assuming that he has the same need to spend lots of time together and that friends play the same part in his life that they do in hers.

While he loves her dearly and is quite willing to ignore his friends while the relationship is getting off the ground (and is aware that his friends do the same thing), his friends only know he is involved because he has been unavailable to them. He feels that to talk about her to them would either be disloyal to her or place too much importance on the relationship. He isn't willing to share her or to announce their engagement, so what's the point? He sure doesn't want anybody bird-dogging her, flirting with her, and he doesn't want them to think that she is a permanent part of his life.

In addition, he is feeling the need to surface just for

a night, to get back to how things were when he was footloose and fancy-free. It's not that he doesn't love her—he just needs some breathing space.

THE RESOLUTION

The hidden agendas in this game are not only different needs for intimacy, and different definitions of friendship, but also different perceptions of trust. She doesn't trust him with his old friends, and he doesn't trust her to make his friends feel welcome in their world. Unfortunately, both have chosen a course that will only exacerbate their mutual distrust. While she doesn't have to love his friends, integrating them into their life will make him feel less stranded, less as though he is having to make sacrifices to be with her. Her perception that his old friends don't like the idea of her and are secretly plotting to split them up by introducing him to other women will make it harder and harder for his two worlds to come together comfortably. He is responsible for his behavior, not the bad influence of his friends.

In trying to possess him and keep him out of harm's way, she is treating him like a naughty little boy, which will only make him feel more isolated and eventually castrated. She needs to have a life outside of their relationship that is fun and functional. If both of them voluntarily and happily both spend and allow the other to spend time with others, time spent together will be better for both.

He needs to understand that friends serve a completely different function in her life, and until she meets his friends, she won't feel that she is really an important part of his life. She would never *not* introduce an important man to her friends, having already spent hours on the phone talking about him to them.

Again, if he doesn't trust his friends not to (1) make a pass, (2) make fun, (3) assume right off he is hopelessly committed and about ready to walk down the aisle, or (4) think he is hopelessly under her thumb, he may have to (1) talk with her about her "public" behavior toward him, (2) look to his own self-confidence, or (3) consider whether these guys are really his friends.

Insecurity about the other's friends bespeaks some insecurity in taking the next step in the relationship, going public. Women are almost always much more willing much sooner to treat a relationship as "important."

The solution to this dilemma is to discuss the underlying issues of trust and of what friends really mean to each, and then to arrange a low-key gathering with some friends of his and some of hers so he can be assured that the scrutiny will be a little less intense and the potential for either serious flirtation or outrageous behavior will be minimized. She can see that his friends aren't animals all dedicated to cajoling him to return to the rolls of randy singles. She needs to make sure that she has a life that goes on independent of him, not only so that he will feel less claustrophobic but for her own sake as well.

He needs to decide whether he really does have male friends who are important to him and who respect him or just a pack of acquaintances who will give him an excuse to be a bad boy.

Family Stuff

♥

THE GAME

They have been dating for three months. His brother, whom she has never met, comes to town, a fact she is apprised of only after the fact. He casually mentions what a good time he and his brother had together and is surprised when she turns icy and says she has to go, that she'll talk to him later. She has invited him numerous times to join her at family gatherings, and he always comes up with an excuse such as work or other social obligations.

THE BLAME

SHE is furious and hurt. How big a deal would it have been for him to invite her along, introduce her? She feels he is treating her like a temporary, sleazy liaison, and she's had about enough. While she doesn't exactly expect him to take her home to meet Mom, she must assume that his reluctance to introduce her to his family or to be introduced to hers is an indication of the instability of their relationship.

HE thinks she's getting a little pushy. What's the big deal? His brother is a jerk anyway, they really don't get along all that well, and while things went okay this visit, if she had been along it would have been awkward and his brother would probably have told embarrassing stories about how scrawny and funny-looking he was as a kid or about old girlfriends, or he might even have made a pass at her. Besides, the relationship isn't that serious yet.

THE EXPLANATION

Both he and she are on the right track, sort of. Men feel being introduced to the family is a major step: they are being put on display and fear that they will be compared to all her other parade of boyfriends and likely be found wanting. She wants to be introduced to his brother for some of the very reasons that strike fear in his heart: permanency, legitimacy, commitment. However, she is used to her family's making comments about her latest, since in the past she was always picked up at the house and her family often met her dates. His family has mostly known when he was involved with somebody new or special only by his frequent absences at meals, in the evenings, or on weekends.

Both are acknowledging the same issues, but they are responding quite differently. The hidden issue here is not necessarily commitment, but competition. He is afraid that he won't measure up and she will be influenced by her parents' disapproval. If he is not committed to her, meeting her family is, in theory, no big deal. Who cares? It is only when he values the relationship that her family's opinion counts.

THE RESOLUTION

She must admit that part of her desire to meet his family is curiosity, but part is an attempt to win them over so she will have allies in his life. But she is missing the point. Commitment has to come from him, not his mother. When he is ready, he will invite her. In the meantime, she may want to downplay the fact that she always brings guys home. If he feels that approval is necessary for the relationship to continue, he is going to be skittish.

If the two of them are sleeping together, he may feel even more reluctant. Once upon a time, a woman's virginity was her family's possession. Marriages were political, and a nonvirgin was significantly less marriageable; loss of virginity could directly affect the family's fortune. While marriages as political alliances are much less common, the leftover feelings aren't. If the relationship is temporary, leaving the family out may be a blessing in the long run. If the relationship gets serious, the family will come into it sooner or later. The introduction of the family does not promote stability, but is the result of stability. Only when both feel that the relationship is strong enough to withstand criticism, commentary, and meddling need the family be involved. If she stops using family gatherings as a barometer, so might he, and meetings might occur later than she would like, but sooner than she anticipated.

Confidentiality

♥

THE GAME

They are having an argument and she points out that when she told Judy about their little problem, Judy confided that she and her boyfriend used to have the same problem and it cleared up in time. He stops dead in his tracks and hollers, "You told Judy? Well, why not just take out an ad in the *News!*" And he storms off.

THE BLAME

HE can't believe she would confide their most intimate secrets, problems or not, to a blabbermouth bubblehead. He feels betrayed and humiliated and is quite sure he can never face Judy, her friends, boyfriends, hairdresser, or anybody in her immediate vicinity ever again and isn't at all sure he wants to continue his current relationship in the first place. Is nothing sacred?

SHE feels that he is only looking for an excuse to walk out, that he is jealous of her friends and the time she spends with them and is always putting them down, making fun of them or trying to avoid them. She knows men have a hard time with feelings, but that's no reason to begrudge her her friendships. She feels that he could definitely benefit from a bit more closeness in his inter-personal dealings. Their relationship might even benefit.

THE EXPLANATION

Again, men and women view friends and friendships in completely different ways; there is almost no overlap. Very few women would think of *not* confiding intimate details of their lives and especially loves to their friends who have seen them through, if not countless, at least many loves and lovers. Women problem-solve by talking and asking and confiding. Men by and large are uncomfortable presenting anything but the most competent face, especially to a friend, especially to another man. The more intimate the problem, the less likely he is to confide. Talking about a problem, especially one that reflects badly on him, he views as betrayal, and since women tend to include their friends more in their couple life, the whole issue of "what she knows" is an ongoing part of his distrust of her friends. If she is foolish enough to confide any criticism or objection or "Sarah doesn't think you're good enough for me," the problem becomes nearly terminal.

THE RESOLUTION

Before this becomes a self-righteous debate on the value of friendships, she might reflect for a moment on how she would feel if he told his friends that she goes most of the winter without shaving her legs, wears knee-highs which he privately refers to as erection killers, or is prone to rude noises after eating too much Jell-O. One of the reasons women can be self-righteous about intimate issues in friendships is that they can feel relatively confident that men don't have friendships based on intimacy, so they can completely finesse the issue of betrayal, confidentiality, and embarrassing secrets.

He might bring this issue to her attention rather than indulging in a tirade about her blabbermouth friends. Without threatening, he could point out, via specific examples, comparable issues.

She might be willing to adopt some ground rules that include (1) not confiding a friend's criticism or comments on intimate secrets, (2) some ground rules for excluded material (3) being reasonable about what SHE would just as soon have remain private if it concerned her. She might also consider being a bit more discreet about her indiscretions. If she's going to blab, she may want to keep silent about blabbing, especially in the middle of an argument that's deteriorating. If it hadn't been deteriorating, she probably wouldn't have been tempted.

It's okay for women to continue to have friendships based on intimacy, but continually complaining about a man's imperfections will probably guarantee a fair amount of hostility between two important people in her life. Vocalizing resentments also gives additional weight to issues that if kept private and quietly analyzed in discussion between the principals might loom less as a battle to the death or a matter of who's right or wrong.

If a man feels that his most intimate thoughts, words, mistakes, or misgivings are going to receive a public airing (and to a man, anybody outside of the two of you is public), he's going to be much less willing to be open. Vulnerability is one thing, public humiliation and ridicule, are quite different.

Working Hard: Priorities

♥

THE GAME

They have been seeing each other steadily for three months. He seems preoccupied and sullen. She is convinced that he's having second thoughts about the relationship and is panicky. She fixes a wonderful dinner and serves his favorite wine, and after a completely successful seduction, she plumps up her pillow and says, "Okay, so now let's talk. Where are we going with this relationship?"

He says, "Look, my ex-wife is making me crazy, my business is in trouble, and I'm not sure where next month's rent is coming from. I just can't deal with this hassle right now."

THE BLAME

HE feels furious, castrated, and betrayed. She has been nagging him for weeks, but he knows that his problems have nothing to do with her and his work needs a lot of attention right now. Why can't she just back off instead of needing constant reassurance that he loves her? She won't love him nearly so much if he's out of work

and can't buy her dinners and trinkets. He was so relieved when she'd seemed calmer this evening and had
been again the lovable woman to whom he'd first become attracted. A great dinner, great sex, and then
wham, out of nowhere, blind-sided again, just when he
was feeling good about at least one area of his life. Why
did she have to go and spoil it?

SHE is fit to be tied. He treats her like a child, assumes
she couldn't understand anything. She too has a job, so
what's the big deal? She tried to do it his way this time—
good dinner, sex, making him feel warm and happy and
loved—and where did it get her? How important can
she really be to him if he's not willing to work on the
relationship? After all, jobs come and go, but she'll always be there for him, so how come he can't get his
priorities straight?

THE EXPLANATION

This is one of those scenarios that painfully points out
the fact that men and women occasionally inhabit different planets. You've heard it a zillion times. You've
even read it here before, but it's impossible to overlook
the truly painful, basic, fundamentally divisive point
that women work at relationships because they consti-
tute the most important single (no pun intended) priority in their lives, whereas men save that distinction for
work. Everything between men and women is destined
to be muddy and angry and unhappy unless this lesson
can be absorbed in the gut and heart as well as the head.

It doesn't mean it's fair or reasonable or even right. Just that it's true and crucial and must be dealt with.

Before we get to the core, we should consider some of the trivial pursuits that are so infuriating along the way.

First, the idea that getting somebody in a good mood is the best way to tackle a difficult problem has some inherent logic, but is exceptionally dangerous in that it sets up the expectation that "she wants something." If indeed she doesn't, the tense anticipation will take the fun out of the moment, and if she does, he feels manipulated.

Second, discussions in bed should probably be saved for completely safe topics. If sex seems to have been used as a pacifier or a tool to get what someone wants, it will taint the pleasure either partner can find in sex.

Third, men feel differently from women about the importance of work in their lives. They have defined themselves by the work they want to do since Cub Scouts. While little girls also talk about being nurses or ballerinas, by adolescence they view their life's work in terms of finding the right man. Men don't view themselves as taking time off from work and career until retirement, so if there's to be an investment of effort, men are usually more apt to put it into work, with relationships coming in a distant second. For women, even if they view themselves as having careers, relationships are the real "business" of life. All of us are usually willing to work hard in some but not all areas of our lives, and when the crunch comes, men are much more likely to work hard at their careers and to want their relationships to be easy. Women feel the opposite, which partially explains why women still make only two thirds of what men make for the same position. This isn't a matter of fairness or rightness, but tradition and socialization. It also explains why how much money a man makes is often an issue in the relationship. He feels that it is important to her because it is important to him.

THE RESOLUTION

The trivialities are easy here, the main issue is not. So we might as well start with the easy stuff. As is true in most things, timing of important discussions is crucial, and her timing stinks. He is right in feeling sandbagged. If she has an important matter to discuss, she should set up a scenario that speaks to important, businesslike, adult issues, not sex. Most discussions are best undertaken with both parties dressed and sober and alert and unhurried. It's okay to say, "Why don't we take a drive out to the country this weekend, so we can get a perspective on our lives and our relationship?" But setting up romantic situations with a sting at the end will make it impossible to have relaxed, romantic situations in the future. Treating a man as if he were a silly mindless infant whose mind turns to mush after sex demeans him and is short-sighted. Pillow talk should probably be limited to things that will make both partners sleep better. Period. Stomach-churning stuff is better dealt with at other times and other places.

Now to the tough stuff. One can't live by constant challenge. If one area of life is treacherous and exciting and uncertain, we usually look for some balancing of security, ease, and comfort in other areas. Conversely, if one area is boring or sedate, effort can easily be expended in other areas. Traditionally men went out and fought saber-toothed tigers and each other and didn't necessarily want to battle the little cave mistress when he got home, so a premium was undoubtedly placed on placid, well-behaved womenfolk.

In the old days, women stayed around taking care of kids and tending gardens and animals, which while time-consuming and exhausting isn't terribly mentally stimulating, so doing something grown-up together— talking, cards, chess, visiting neighbors, home improvements—seemed sort of fun when the provider got home. (This is fairly recent history. Ancient history didn't provide much light, time, energy, diversions, or longevity for much other than survival and sleep.)

While many women work these days, undoing centuries of conditioning doesn't come quickly or easily, and society still gives a somewhat mixed message about women's *real* work. In their attempt to be superwomen, many women are giving tacit approval to the notion that the important issue in their lives is family, not work, or work only if family is going well.

Women need a focus separate from domestic concerns so as not to become isolated or bereft. Men undoubtedly need to balance work concerns with more of an investment in their own emotional lives, which quickly comes down to relationships. The trap for both is the traditional expectations surrounding work and money. She may have to contribute more money and allow him to contribute less or the workplace will continue to hold sway.

For this couple, he needs to decide whether this relationship is important enough to make it as much of a priority as his work. If it is not, he needs to tell her, and if it is, he should be more open about his work preoccupation and invest more time and effort in their shared lives.

She needs to reexamine her attitude toward work, and if she is just viewing it as a holding action until he takes her away from it all, then she has to stop equating it with his work. He's playing for keeps, she's just playing for time. If her work is crucial to her, she needs to find a man who cares as much about juggling priorities as she does, but she must be willing to put her paycheck where her principles are—to pay half, or at least her share, at all times rather than give him the mixed message that they're equal partners when it suits her but not when it comes out of her pocket.

Mind vs. Body

♥

THE GAME

He comes over for the evening. She has set the scene with candlelight and wine and soft music. She is wearing his favorite dress and has cooked all of his favorite things. After dinner, she snuggles up to him and says, "Let's talk." He gets amorous, and when she resists his advances, he increases his ardor. He begins to get a bit miffed when he realizes that she's truly not interested. He finally gets sullen, won't meet her eyes, and completely ignores her tears as she sobs dejectedly that he won't ever listen to her.

THE BLAME

SHE says he never takes her seriously, won't talk to her, and isn't interested in her as a person. She also really wants him to clarify for her what's going on in the relationship, how he feels about her, about them, and how serious he is about their future. But since he's so reluctant to talk about it she always finds herself lecturing him, nagging, or whining. And while she hates herself for it, she could use some reassurance. She thought if she could soften him up a bit, maybe he'd be in a good mood or at least be pleased that she'd done so many

86

things to please him and would treat her with some respect instead of just wanting to hit the sheets.

HE feels he's been had. Is she just testing her power over him or what? And this constant talking—she says talk, but what she really means is bitch. Whenever they "talk" she ends up crying, and he ends up apologizing, although he's never sure for what, exactly.

He's delighted that she's gone to so much trouble to please him. Dinner was great, she looks and smells wonderful, and he just meant to show his appreciation. And now look what happened. No matter what he does, it's never right.

He is not completely stupid, but is tired of the same old where-do-we-go-from-here speech. He really does care about her, but she can't argue him into loving her, and sometimes he just gets tired of talking about things. Besides, she doesn't really want to hear what he is feeling, she just wants to hear that he is feeling the same thing she is feeling. He thought that this evening was a vacation from the serious stuff and he was delighted to take her up on her invitation, and now she's mad again.

THE EXPLANATION

She figured the best way to a man's heart is through his stomach, but she's aiming higher and he's aiming lower. If she wants to have a businesslike discussion, she needs to give him the appropriate clues, which definitely do *not* include soft lights and shoulders. It doesn't mean she has to be dressed in banker's gray, but a lunch date in a quiet, nonsexy restaurant when both of them have some time to talk—which may mean a nonwork day— might be a more appropriate setting than a sexy boudoir. She's sending a mixed message. She is trying to sugar-coat what she assumes are her unpalatable demands. If it's time for a showdown, think John Wayne, not Madonna.

He is responding to the stimuli with which he feels more comfortable, and by her tactics, she is offering that option. It's not that he doesn't know what's bugging her, but if he brings it up, she'll pounce on it and treat him like a two-year-old, or if he brings up something that's not bugging her, it gives her new fodder. So he's best off playing dumb. Besides, he thought maybe she was just being nice, and if she wasn't, maybe he could distract her from talking.

THE RESOLUTION

She must stop pulling her punches. If she needs to know if he's serious, if they're going to get married, does his mother like her, a pot roast is not the way to get an answer. Ask him. If she's thinking about viewing him as a lifetime commitment, it's high time to get in the habit of asking or saying what's on her mind. If he doesn't volunteer, the only way to get the information is to ask for it, loud and clear with no chance for mis-interpretation or ducking. If she wants a serious dis-cussion, she shouldn't dress for a seduction, and if she's given the same speech to him more than a few times before, she should either change the speech or give up the tactic. If something hasn't worked half a dozen times before, the chance of it working this time is between slim and none.

If she's got a specific complaint, she should voice it clearly and succinctly, and stay current. Old issues aren't going to be resolved if they haven't been in several earlier attempts, and they take on the feeling of folklore after a while. Most adults aren't crazy about lectures from other adults, especially in intimate relationships.

He could take a bit more responsibility for what's going on between the two of them and stop playing dumb or acting the naughty child to her stern mother. If nothing else, it might stop the lectures. When he knows that he's made her unhappy and knows why, an apology is in order. When he's not sure, genuinely not sure, it's okay to ask, especially if he's occasionally 'fessed up in the past. If he's truly befuddled, assuming it doesn't happen all the time, he should be willing to listen. Getting used to complaining is often the first step to getting in touch with feelings in a relationship. But both parties have to be willing to listen, to be as nondefensive as possible, to talk, and most important, either to change behavior or admit that change is unlikely. Otherwise the same old issues will constantly recur.

Good communication requires that an individual know what he or she is feeling, be able to conceptualize it, verbalize it in a way the other is likely to understand, then wait for the entire process to occur in reverse. In addition to being moderately conversant with feelings, both parties have to be willing to listen long and well enough to get beyond the obvious and the historical. Since communication is not easy to begin with, giving mixed messages is just going to increase the possibility of being misunderstood. No sandbagging, no seduction, just courage and simplicity, time and patience, an open heart and open mind.

The Third Category

♥

THE GAME

They've been dating steadily for three months. Her mother is getting antsy, her friends want to know if this is "the one." She likes being with him, they laugh a lot together, the sex is great, neither is seeing anybody else. Valentine's Day is coming up. She finally gets up her nerve and says, "Okay, where do we go from here?" He said, "What do you mean? Things are fine just the way they are. Why do you want to spoil everything?"

THE BLAME

SHE is not getting any younger, and she doesn't want to waste any more time with him if this relationship isn't going anywhere. They do have a great time together and maybe it's a little soon to think about getting engaged, but it would be nice if he would at least suggest moving in together. She is feeling the pressure from all sides to firm this thing up, but mostly she wonders if he plans to go on using her as a security blanket, a teddy bear, until she is old and gray and beyond childbearing, and then to go find a young good-looking bimbo to raise scores of babies while she grows old alone.

HE feels like she thinks she can talk him into loving her. He does like her, doesn't feel the need of another woman, but is sure that she is *not* the one. He can't say exactly why, but he knows that one of these days, he will meet the right woman. But she's just fine until that day comes. He doesn't want to make her unhappy and they are having a good time together, so what's the big deal? He doesn't need to *talk* about the *relationship* all the time. Let's just enjoy a good thing for as long as it lasts, he thinks.

THE EXPLANATION

Women have basically two categories for a man: acceptable and unacceptable. While it may take a while to figure out where he fits, once he's categorized, it's either dump him or let's get on with the relationship, step by step.

Men have a third category. In addition to the ones that have no place in his life and the right one, there are those who are good enough until the right one comes along, who are in a sort of holding pattern.

The other factor that has to be considered is that men and women have different attitudes toward love at first sight. At some primitive level, love at first sight is hormones with possibilities. It is visual, sexual, and quick, all qualities that men appreciate. While a woman might find herself instantly attracted, her conditioning will guide her at least to consider other factors, such as power, personality, child-rearing potential, income, and manners. The initial criteria for men in choosing a woman are some combination of visual and sexual. While he might later be influenced by other factors, the first rush is physical attraction.

Once these two factors of a male belief in a third category in the possibility of rounding the next corner and being struck dumb are understood, a lot of seemingly senseless and insensitive behavior becomes painfully clear. Those anguished cries from women—"He is never willing to talk about *us*"—make a bit more sense. However, there are in fact numerous reasons that a man may be unwilling to talk about relationship-type stuff. He may feel that it really isn't important, he may find it too scary, he may think it's only an excuse for her to bitch, he may think she doesn't want to hear what he has to say anyway, he may be uncomfortable talking about feelings, or he may think she twists his words and he always comes out the bad guy.

These reasons are difficult but fixable. Consignment to a third category isn't fixable, because it presupposes that one person is committed to going to the next step and the other is committed to going to the next relationship. And that's not really negotiable.

This third category also explains why a woman will say she's involved when a friend offers to fix her up or an old flame comes to town, while her male counterpart is equally likely to say that yes he's dating, but he's really not seeing anybody special. Also an old flame may be more of a threat to her than the comparable relationship might be to him. Since he's always looking, not sure that she's *it*, he's always open to a new experience or woman while waiting to be thunderstruck by the right woman, even while walking down the aisle.

Sooner or later, a man will succumb. But from a lot of confused and hurt women's point of view, usually not until his legs are about to give out. At which time he will convince himself that the next bimbette to walk through the door is *her* and fall madly in love or at least convince himself he has, often by simply letting go of the idea that the next one lurking around the corner would be at all interested in him. She may or may not be appropriate, in love with him, after his money, ready to settle down, wishing to have children, etc.

THE RESOLUTION

Unless she is willing to be incredibly passive and wait till he decides where he is in the relationship, she is best off being very honest in terms of what she really wants. Many women today really want to get married but are unwilling to admit it, so they hide behind ideas like commitment and the biological time clock and men who are really boys and guys who are looking for mothers rather than wives. But those reasons are irrelevant. If she decides that she is willing to settle for the relationship as it currently exists, then she shouldn't worry about the M word. If she is unwilling to continue if it's certain the relationship will never be any more than it currently is, she should tell him. Not threaten him, but tell him so that she can make her decision and leave. The tricky part is the middle ground. She's currently happy but is unwilling to wait forever. She then has to decide how long she is willing to wait and tell him.

He might try being very honest about his feelings not only with her but with himself. The fantasy that the right woman will suddenly materialize is perhaps even more dangerous to a man than the companion fantasy is to a woman, because he will often involve himself in a relationship that is going nowhere while he is waiting for someone else. Saying "I will never marry you because you are not what I want" may seem callous in the short run but would save both of them a lot of teary, guilt-infested, gut-wrenching sessions. If she stays, it's because she is harboring no illusions. In the meantime, he might be alone, but alone is often a lot better place to be if you are really serious about looking for the right one.

Falling in love is not a conscious decision, although allowing ourselves to fall may be. Nobody is responsible for falling in love with one person or another, but once in love, we are responsible for how we behave. A woman can decide to settle for less than she thought she wanted, or not. A man can decide to embrace whole-heartedly what he thinks of as a compromise and be content or not if he is willing to decide that the third category is the Tooth Fairy and the Easter Bunny and Santa Claus—i.e., a short-term, feel-good fantasy—and get on with the business of reality. It is crucial to be honest not only with a partner, but even more important with oneself.

Honesty is a bit rough on everybody, especially in a society that is so fond of romantic illusions, but it saves a lot of wear and tear in the long run.

Sex Too Soon

♥

THE GAME

They were introduced by their banker when he was overdrawn and she wanted to see about a car loan. They went out for coffee, continued into dinner, and spent the entire evening talking their heads off, noting their similar taste in movies, food, friends, and detergents. He asked for a date the following week; they had another relaxed, wonderful dinner. He asked what she was doing Saturday night, she said nothing and invited him to her place for dinner. After consuming a good bottle of Beaujolais that he had brought, they retired between pasta and dessert to the bedroom. The sex was as good as the dinner. She phoned all her friends the next day to tell them she had finally met Mr. Right. As the weeks wore on without a phone call, she began to wonder whether she had imagined the whole thing.

THE BLAME

HE really liked her and felt she was something special, and really meant to call her, but there seemed to be all sorts of excuses for not doing so. Admittedly, he would have liked to wait a bit longer to hit the sheets and to pick the time and place. He believes in liberated women and all of that, but she moved faster than he anticipated. He wonders whether she moves this fast with all her guys.

SHE feels that these days if a woman doesn't move fast the guy will move on. She felt he was a classier guy than a slam-bam, thank you ma'am, but she's been fooled before. They had so much in common, she felt that they were soulmates, and she wishes now that she had been able to see through his disguise more quickly and saved herself the heartache.

THE EXPLANATION

Neither he nor she was ready to have sex yet. Even at the end of the twentieth century, most men still view themselves as the pursuers. You can't turn back overnight thousands of years of conditioning. Man once thought of himself as the only one with sexual desires. This assumption allowed him the luxury of checking out only his own equipment before deciding whether or not to pursue his lady love. If he'd had a little too much to drink or a hard day at the Crusades, he could just roll over and shine it on, cheerfully taking for granted that his woman was only obliging him to be friendly. Sex was his need, not hers.

The events in her bedroom while pleasant at the time, do make him feel a bit off balance and not in control, since he hadn't planned to seduce her for at least two or three more dates. In the sexual arena, this means trouble for all but the most secure male (who probably exists only in *Cosmo* fiction or Alan Alda movies). The initiative has been snatched from his sweaty palms, and while everything worked out okay this time, what about next time?

THE RESOLUTION

Getting to know each other with clothes on allows for a realistic assessment with heads as well as hearts and other organs, and neither is put in the position of having to explain terror or commitment. Nobody has to justify anything. He can talk about his old-fashioned ideas or his need for control or even his fear about not being able to perform. She can discuss her wish to please him and her concern that it not be at the expense of her own instincts or vulnerability.

Women, don't have sex until you can accept it for exactly what it is: the moment, not a commitment. If you'll be devastated if he doesn't call the next day, keep your feet on the floor and your zipper up, and make sure your head is engaged. Men, unless you want to go through life feeling like a user, know her middle name and remember she has a heart that is every bit as vulnerable and tender as whatever organ you're presently contemplating. If you get to know her, you may not feel so infatuated, but you may also be less likely to view her as a patsy and yourself as a heel. Biology seems to have conditioned women to try to ensnare a man by doing it "his way" and men to be ever willing, eager, priapic, and unable to say no. These patterns are incompatible, slightly silly, and dangerous.

However, the situation isn't inevitable or hopeless. Both sexes have this wonderful big fat cortex sitting on top of all those other organs. Each can think, assess his or her own motives honestly, and communicate to the other without damage to either ego. It is okay for *either* to say no.

Men and women don't have to view each other as natural enemies, even though we all tend to act in characteristic ways that we have been conditioned to by our moms, *Playboy*, society, our health teacher, Sunday school, or giggly friends and smutty TV programs. We can be nice human beings even while we are responding to our juices or destiny.

While sex is a perfectly good part of a relationship, it does tend to move us at the speed of light past some things that we perhaps shouldn't be moving past at all, let alone at that speed and in opposite directions (the women feeling more committed and vulnerable, the man feeling either out of control or in complete control, neither of which is particularly the case early on.) Good sex is based on closeness and intimacy if it is to be more than organ pleasure, and intimacy requires openness and a willingness to let ourselves be vulnerable, which requires trust. And trust takes time. No satisfactory shortcuts have been discovered to date. Stay tuned for further developments in the next several thousand years.

Sexual Stereotyping

♥

THE GAME

They've had a lovely evening together. She's a bit ambivalent about the next step and has just about decided that waiting to invite him up makes some sense. Then he announces that he really needs to use her bathroom. Once upstairs, when he's out of the bathroom, it seems only hospitable to offer him a cup of coffee, and then he has to drink it, and all of a sudden they seem to be locked in a fairly passionate embrace. While her resolve is failing, she has enough presence of mind between kisses to say somewhat breathlessly that while she would like to have him spend the night, she isn't ready to make love. He agrees that it sounds like a great idea to just cuddle. They get ready for bed, and her chaste good-night kiss turns into something a bit more passionate, and since she always has condoms in the bedside drawer, they somehow end up making love. The next morning both sort of wish they'd waited just a bit longer.

THE BLAME

SHE feels like a slut. He obviously had no intention of keeping his word, and she will most likely never hear from him again. If she does, it's probably because he just figures she's easy. Both her self-respect and her respect for him (he seemed nicer than those other guys) have plummeted, and the incident has reconfirmed what she already suspected and her mother already knew: they're all beasts.

HE is confused but fairly content. She seemed sort of stand-offish earlier in the evening, but she obviously wanted it even though he would have preferred to have waited, since he has a busy day ahead and is a little unsure about where they go from here. He hadn't been that convinced that he was going to go out with her again. She seems perfectly nice, but he's not really in the market for an intense relationship, and she's either this easy with everyone or she's really got it bad for him. He feels he's damned if he does, damned if he doesn't. In fact, he has felt that way from the moment he asked to use her bathroom. After all, a fellow has to try so she won't think he's gay, and that jazz about sleeping together with no sex—who does she think she's kidding? He just got a little carried away, but she seems none the worse for wear.

THE EXPLANATION

The *Playboy* philosophy has done its best to poison relationships between men and women by implying that any man worth the name is ever ready to nail any woman at any time and any woman (or at least girl) worth the name needs to be sweet-talked into bed. And while she really wants it, she'll never admit it, so it's a matter of seducing her, conning her, and then assuring her you respect her in the morning, even if you think she's either loose (if she wants "it") or stupid and gullible (if she doesn't but gets talked into it).

Men feel that everybody expects them to be ever horny and ready. And no matter what a man does, it's wrong. If he doesn't make a pass it's because he really prefers boys or finds her unattractive (maybe because he unconsciously prefers boys?). At least making a pass means that he may get some action, even if he runs the risk of making a fool of himself and being rejected.

She mirrors his fears. If he behaves, is he a gentleman, uninterested, gay, or feeling some momentary guilt toward an absent wife or girlfriend whom he has neglected to mention? If he does make a pass, is it to notch his belt or bolster his ego, or just because he feels it's expected? If she succumbs, will he perceive her as horny, eager, loose, or stupid? If he doesn't call, is it because she wasn't very good, was too eager, wasn't eager enough, was a one-night-stand from the beginning, or just wasn't the type?

What a mess.

THE RESOLUTION

I know I'm beginning to sound like your great-Aunt Gertrude, but waiting to hit the sheets until both of you feel comfortable enough to talk about what the experience means to both of you can save an awful lot of wear and tear on ego, conscience, and reputation, both his and hers. Sex really does mean different things to different people, and any meaning is probably okay as long as it is communicated and understood. If both are out to party naked, so be it. If one wants a phone call the next day, it's best to say so ahead of time and see if some pattern of phone interaction has been previously established. Neither party can positively guarantee the outcome of a sexual encounter, but a little consumer awareness can go a long way. Discussing expectations ahead of time may be the ultimate not only in foreplay, but in very satisfying oral sex. Both partners may not only actually get what they want, but feel good in the process—before, during, and especially after. Admittedly, the before may feel a bit awkward, but that is a reasonable price to pay for a cheerful during and a comfortable, nonambiguous, guilt-free after.

Pursuit

THE GAME

They were introduced by a mutual friend, and it wasn't love at first sight. She immediately noticed his bald spot, protruding teeth, and weak chin. He seemed much more interested in her than she in him. He called her up and asked her out, and when she said she was busy, he just kept on asking. She finally gave in, because there wasn't anybody else in the picture and he had gotten tickets for a good concert and besides he seemed terribly interested in her, so she figured why not give him a second chance. He continued to pursue her; she continued to turn down more dates than she accepted. He took her to nice places and was very attentive.

After several months, she decided he was awfully nice, although her girlfriends kept reminding her of the physical imperfections she had laughingly enumerated after their first date. She finally succumbed to his ardent and passionate entreaties and spent the night with him. The next day, she breathlessly confided to her girlfriends that she might have found the guy for her. When they suggested that she might want to leave the line free for his phone call, she assured them that he would keep trying till he got hold of her.

After two weeks of silence, she began to suspect that something terrible had happened to him. She called him at work. He was embarrassingly curt on the phone, saying he had been really busy, but would call soon. She never heard from him again.

THE BLAME

HE doesn't really divide the world into good women and not-so-good women; it's just that he was getting to know her and for some reason that's not altogether clear to him, she just doesn't seem as special as she once did. He really did intend to get back in touch with her, but it kind of slipped his mind, and then when he thought about it, he realized that it had been a while since he talked to her and he was embarrassed to call after all that time had gone by. Whenever she crosses his mind, he feels a bit embarrassed, but he thinks highly of her and would say so if anybody asked.

SHE feels she's been had. She really liked him; there aren't that many guys that she would invite into her apartment, let alone into her bed. To think he viewed her as a one-night stand is humiliating and infuriating. She views him as one more of those bun-and-run guys who only thinks about scoring. Besides, who the hell is he to have the nerve not to call her so that she can tell him that she'll never go out again with a creep like him?

THE EXPLANATION

A well-known comedian has declared that the best time in a relationship for a man is just before he and his new girlfriend have gone to bed together. He tells all of his friends how pretty she is, how special, how sweet, how unlike any other woman he's ever dated before, how pretty her hair, how cute her figure. Finally he gets her to bed, and discovers immediately after he comes that she has a dead tooth.

When a woman first meets a man, she is very likely going to notice his knobby knees, his receding hairline and chin, his shabby cuffs. Once she finally succumbs and goes to bed with him, she notices his dead tooth, but is a firm believer in cosmetic dentistry. Both are going at the speed of light in completely opposite directions, and we wonder why the war between the sexes has yet to cool down.

He is intent upon the challenge. As long as she is unobtainable, beyond his grasp, she is heavenly and desirable. Once she has given in, the challenge has been met; she is his and her specialness evaporates. He can view her as not only ordinary, but flawed. This may be a subtle variation on the Groucho Marx philosophy— "Who'd want to join a club that would have somebody like me as a member?" His insecurities about himself are transferred onto her shoulders, or in this case, her dental work.

She is going in the opposite direction. Her initial reluctance, based on a graphic and somewhat cruel description of his flaws, allowed her to remain aloof, protected, and uninvolved, which only served to increase his ardor. She begins to feel that she really is special to him and therefore is more closely bound than she thought, so it is okay to allow him under her skin, literally and figuratively. Once she has done so, she needs to justify her own vulnerability by making him not only okay, but desirable. Hence the proliferation of one-night stands and broken hearts and increasingly cynical men who view women as clingy and needy, and clingy, needy, cynical women who view all men as only interested in one thing.

She has participated in her own downfall by presenting herself as a challenge, by buying into his feelings rather than her own, and on a less than wholesome level, by being willing to use him as an escort without having any real interest in him.

He hasn't covered himself with glory either. Consciously or unconsciously he has set either himself or her up. If she really isn't interested in him, why the masochism? If he just intends to "get" her, and then drop her as soon as she's gotten, why the sadism? Sexual revenge isn't pretty, regardless of the sex of the perpetrator or victim. Everybody loses unless belt notching or bruised hearts are the object of the exercise.

THE RESOLUTION

Believe it or not, the solution isn't for men to be less charming and ardent and women to be less vulnerable, although that's not a bad place to start. It's that both men and women must be a bit more realistic and informed about the possible object of their desire.

If she doesn't like him, she shouldn't go out with him regardless of the relentless nature of his pursuit.

He needs to decide whether he is truly interested in her as a person rather than as an elusive trophy.

Admittedly, it is sometimes difficult to gauge interest

early in a relationship, but if the words "milk of magnesia" occur to her when his name is mentioned or "bitch goddess" to him when picturing her face, perhaps both should think again. He could take his hunting instincts out on sataris, computer arcades, mystery novels, or fake war games rather than fellow human beings.

She might think in terms of a lapdog if she is seeking adoration without vulnerability or commitment. Both might ask of themselves whether they would be interested in the characteristics of the other if they were demonstrated in a friend. If the answer is no, perhaps both should politely and quickly, although gently, exit the relationship and the temptation to play such a dangerous game.

Sex is complicated enough when both people genuinely like each other. To sleep with someone out of curiosity or boredom, or because you've been worn down by relentless pursuit, or because you think it's your obligation, is unwise, tacky, and usually disastrous.

Flowers

♥

THE GAME

It's her first day at a new job, and a gorgeous bouquet complete with a Mylar balloon has just been delivered to her desk. Everybody is crowding around as she opens the envelope. She is hoping his message on the florist card won't be too suggestive to read. She turns the card over: "Best of luck to the first female chairman-of-the-board-to-be." It is signed, "Mom." When he picks her up after work and asks how her first day went, she is barely civil.

THE BLAME

HE can't figure out what's bugging her. While he knows that first days are hard, he expected her to be pleased and happy. He thinks maybe she's about to get her period. When he mentions this she snaps his head off and then retreats into moody silence. He honestly has no idea of the problem.

SHE feels that he takes neither her nor her accomplishments seriously, or is subtly undermining her career, or just doesn't care about her. In a moment of lucidity, she realizes she may be making a mountain out of a molehill, but if her mother could understand how important the first day at her new job is to her, why couldn't he? He obviously knows he should have sent flowers and is just playing dumb so he won't have to admit his mistake.

THE EXPLANATION

There really are at least three problems here. First, the difference between how men and women see work. Second, the nature of celebration. Third, the dangers of assuming if your mother knows, so will your lover. And then there is the role of flowers in a woman's life. Since the first three are tackled at other points in the book, let's look at the whole issue of flowers here.

If you are a man, you might be tempted to turn the page, failing to understand why such a topic would even be included. Do so only at your own peril. There really is a point to all of this.

Most of the differences in male and female perceptions that are discussed in this book can be diagrammed and discussed logically. This is one that just *is*. Whether you call it tradition, romanticism, sentimentality, or craziness, it's one of those facts that have to be accepted on faith by men, but are terribly valuable—as is much such arcane, secret wisdom.

For men, flowers are for special occasions: weddings, funerals, birthdays, anniversaries, Valentine's Day, Mother's Day. Influenced by FTD, the assumption is the bigger and more lavish the better. Fellows, trust me on this one. Flowers for no reason at all are probably your single most effective investment per dollar spent that can be made. The corollary is also true: the absence of flowers for important (to her mind) events is one of the most costly errors per dollar you can make. If men were really aware of the emotional impact of flowers on a woman, they might consider putting their friendly neighborhood florist on retainer.

Actually, the neighborhood florist is not even necessary—the neighborhood greengrocer will do. Not only is lavish and expensive *not* the point, but small, sentimental, and handpicked may be better. Roses are very costly, but one perfect long-stemmed white may be more effective than half a dozen red. A violet nosegay may work better than a chrysanthemum centerpiece, unless you've been invited to Thanksgiving dinner at her parents' house. The point of a flower to a woman is that it says, "You're special"—so it follows that the more romantic, the more unusual and special (not necessarily the more expensive), the better. Although overwhelming is also nice occasionally, gobs of tulips or daisies or anything make a lovely romantic gesture. The unexpected is terrific. The gesture is part of the act. Having them delivered is fine, and there is something very sexy about long white boxes, but showing up with them is also lovely, so you can experience the pleasure firsthand. Sending flowers to the office carries the additional benefit of a public display of affection.

One of the difficulties of accepting something like this on blind faith is that it's necessary to memorize the rules. However, a few logical points come to mind. If flowers have always been used in a traditional way—for instance as an apology—in the past, it is unwise to send them for no reason without explanation. A thoughtful, loving gesture might be construed as a making-up gesture for some as-yet-undiscovered sin. At least have sense enough not to send the same kind you used for guilt.

While convention suggests that flowers go from male to female, many men when forced against a wall will blushingly admit that they too appreciate flowers for the same reason women do. Perhaps because they serve no function except to beautify, flowers are viewed as romantic, unexpected, and kind of sexy, although pretzels or chocolate-chip cookies delivered in a florist's box may work just as well. Most men would prefer flowers that don't suggest that they might come out of the closet at any moment. Think in terms of mums, calla lilies—anything but long-stemmed roses or violet nosegays.

Men also tend to take themselves very seriously at work, so be a little careful of potentially embarrassing gestures there. Males and females really do see the world differently. What would be thrilling to receive if you're a woman might be embarrassing or compromising or silly if you're a man at work. Perhaps subtlety is in order. In lieu of a flamboyant gesture, try something sexy, hidden. Something delivered in a plain brown wrapper, a note in his lunch bag or briefcase, assuming his secretary doesn't unload his briefcase or the guys tease him if his lunchbox smells like Chanel V or the note isn't likely to fall out in the middle of an important meeting, can also be enticing. A boutonniere or a plant might work better. Besides, the point of this whole section is that men and women view flowers differently. You are trying to remind someone you care about that you're thinking of him or her. It's the unexpected, romantic gestures that aren't public but are thoughtful and warm and caring that turn all of us on.

Even with flowers, it's possible to get into a rut and thereby blunt the effectiveness of the gesture. If flowers have become an expected gift, try giving something else or another arrangement or a different kind of flower.

Form is as important as function. I was once married to a man who brought flowers home every Friday night and put them on the counter. He didn't unwrap them or put them in a vase, or hand them to me; he just put them on the counter. A romantic gesture has to have some follow-through. It can't be perfunctory. Getting taken for granted isn't sexy or romantic, and neither are mixed messages. The focus of a romantic gesture is a statement saying "I value you," not "Look at what I've done."

THE RESOLUTION

If she could help him to understand how much romantic gestures mean in an abstract way, perhaps she could allow him enough leeway to figure out how to put his own stamp on flowers, chocolates, cards, or whatever. If she decides that if he really loved her, he'd know, they and the relationship are all in trouble.

Perhaps every woman could take it upon herself to educate one friend—not lover, but friend—into the mysterious ways of flower giving, so sooner or later all the lovers in the world would know.

In the meantime, if she could explain her feelings without calling him a clod or herself a fool, he might get the point and take her out for a special dinner, or recite poetry or send her flowers in the next week or two for no good reason at all. It may be that women are to flowers as men are to cigars: some things are mysterious, unknowable, and they require a leap of fate. That's just the way it is.

Lying

THE GAME

She has just bought a new dress and asks how he likes it. He says it looks terrific on her. Several weeks later, he is planning to take her to dinner with his boss and asks her specifically not to wear the aforementioned dress. When she asks why, he says it makes her look like one of the elephants in tutus from *Fantasia*. She decides that she never wants to see him again. She asked, he lied, then insulted her. If he'd lie about this, then where's the limit?

THE BLAME

HE is more than astounded by her behavior. She takes everything so seriously. He doesn't even remember saying he liked the dress before, and if he did, it was probably because they were late or he wasn't paying much attention or because she never really cares what he says anyway as long as he just tells her she looks nice. He probably said it just before they walked into the party so she'd feel pretty and confident. Besides, when he is honest with her, she either bursts into tears or argues with him or tells him he doesn't know anything about fashion.

. . .

SHE wonders how many other times he has lied where he's said he liked the way she looked or something she had cooked. And has he said he loved her and not really meant it? She is honest with him, and both of them have had a good laugh at the expense of some of his outrageous ties. She bought the dress because she thought he'd like it; she spent too much money and would never have picked it out just for herself. And if he didn't like it, well, she could have returned it and gotten her money back and bought something at least one of them liked. She really dresses to please him, so if he's not honest, what's the use?

THE EXPLANATION

This particular problem has to do not only with lying, but more significantly with truth. Between outright lying and truth-telling for most men is the huge gray area of flattery, silence, and diplomacy. The assumption here is that "nobody will be hurt," which may be true for the short term, but women, perhaps because they invest more in what a man thinks, will often take his words more seriously, or at least take them more seriously when they hear what they want to hear. Flattery and diplomacy depend on a willing participant—one willing to suspend disbelief in the service of hearing what she wants to hear. Men tend to treat women like children and will lie to them about the same kinds of things and for the same reasons: to offer comfort, for expediency, or because they simply don't have an opinion. All of us believe what we want to believe. It is difficult to flatter or deceive someone who is clear about his or her own worth, body, mind, wardrobe, warts, and beauty spots. All of which still leaves us with the slightly less palatable issue of what constitutes a lie and the motive behind its telling.

To be brutal, men and women lie about different things. Men will lie about the future. They will lie when they are sexually aroused—to themselves as well as to her—if it means getting her into bed. As the song says, he never made her any promises, at least, none she'd expect him to keep. Women will also lie to themselves when aroused about their own or his motives. It's just that they lie about different things: their age, weight, whether they really want to get married, how independent they are.

Hormones and honesty are very likely mutually incompatible. Most men and probably most women will lie to save face, and to avoid hurting someone's feelings.

Obviously, you can't be honest with somebody else if you're not honest with yourself. How can you convey the truth if you don't know it?

Broccoli is a great example of men's and women's different perceptions of honesty. A woman will tell a perfect stranger that he has broccoli between his front teeth. A man will not tell his bride on their honeymoon that she's had broccoli lodged in her pearly whites since the rehearsal dinner.

THE RESOLUTION

Women, don't constantly look to him to reassure you about your own worth, beauty, and virtue. Your opinion counts as much as if not more than his. Let him offer compliments spontaneously rather than in response to your fishing for them. And be willing to hear his criticism as honest concern rather than chilling, caustic, hurtful undermining. (If you really believe that he's out to get you, why the hell are you with him, for heaven's sake?)

You will be much less prone to being deceived if you're not constantly asking for reassurance and are not unwilling to take criticism. You're a grown-up, not a child who will be blown away by anything less than resounding praise.

Men, your role is not to be a yes man. You're entitled to an opinion. You wouldn't deceive people at work if you valued your own integrity. Think of how you view apple polishers at the office. You're creating a foundation of quicksand if you can't be honest in an intimate relationship. Your opinion counts, and you count. Don't fritter away your own credibility.

In this particular situation, she needs to stop asking for compliments and reassurance and he needs to offer opinions on things that are important to him. (Both need to understand that the other will probably consider different things to be important.) Sharing that information is called good communication. Expecting the other to take seriously the things you think are important by reading your mind leads to major-league fights.

She needs to show gratitude when he is willing to be

honest with her about things that are important to him. She needs to be more accepting, even when it's painful, if she really wants honesty, not flattery. He may need to learn a bit of gentleness in offering his negative opinions and to be sure that he's equally honest and forthcoming about compliments. It doesn't have to be on a one-for-one basis, but on the basis that he is aware and willing to communicate about what's true and real—both the positive and the negative.

Women, if you ever find a guy who tells you about the mustard at the corner of your mouth or the broccoli in your front teeth and you're not in the middle of a ferocious argument, grab him and hang on for dear life. Unless *all* he does is comment on the negative, you've got a good one.

Changing Levels of Commitment

THE GAME

They met at a party; they both work in the city. He lives in the burbs, she lives in the city, so they've been spending most nights at her apartment. She hints that she'd like to see where he lives. They agree she'll come for the weekend. They've arranged to spend some time with mutual friends and go for a long drive in the country before descending on what he cheerfully describes as his "hovel." The weekend has been relaxed and affectionate and companionable. They finally end up back at his place where he has obviously scurried around cleaning up. She goes into the bathroom and notices grunge behind the water faucets and reads him the riot act, which culminates in her hollering, "How can I hang out with a man who can't even clean a bathroom properly?"

THE BLAME

HE thinks she's way out of line. She's the one who wanted to see his place—well, okay, technically, he was tired of being on her turf all the time too. He's not a professional maid, but he cleaned the place up for her.

No matter what he does, she's always finding fault. He knows his place is a dump and not as nice as hers, but she doesn't have to rub his nose in it. Besides, is a little bathroom grunge all that crucial?

SHE wonders how big a deal it is to spend more than five minutes cleaning up the place. She always makes sure her place is spotless for him, and she knows he's busy, but how long does it take to clean a bathroom properly? Sometimes she feels as if he's fifteen and she's his mom telling him how to do things properly and he's trying to get her goat by screwing up. She knows she overreacted a bit, but it really bothers her that he's such a slob.

THE EXPLANATION

Before we look at the bathroom question, it's important to remember that men and women have been taught to view domesticity in completely different terms. We question the very masculinity of a man who is too fastidious about his home (the pad of a raging heterosexual is supposed to be adorably messy so some very domestic woman can feel needed, at least according to Hollywood). A woman's nesting instincts and therefore the core of her femininity is suspect if she is not punctilious enough in her maidenly duties. Even if his place looks like World War III, a man will seldom do more than hurriedly move a pile of rubble out of the way while declaring that it's the maid's day off. A woman will apologize for the unkemptness of a place that would pass for an operating room. However, this particular blame game has a lot less to do with different standards of tidiness than with unspoken expectations.

When an affair has been taking place almost entirely on one person's turf, the curiosity about the other's space is often more about what that person is withholding or hiding; it's curiosity about the person, not the space.

Both he and she were a bit nerved up about the unveiling. He probably did his best, although he may have felt that a bit of dirt might be a reasonable distraction to his relatively humble digs, and that she wasn't going to approve anyhow, so to hell with a really good cleaning job. All of which goes a long way to explain his and her reactions, but not the vehemence.

By allowing her to see his place, he was signaling that the relationship was moving forward, and by her curiosity and polite but firm insistence, she was acknowledging the step. Neither of them dealt with the issue straightforwardly, perhaps because neither of them was consciously aware of its importance. He sees the experience as a test of whether she accepts him and his lifestyle. So, unfortunately, does she, and to her, his failure to clean a bathroom properly may mean that he doesn't really love her, and even more terrifyingly, that he may not be able to take care of himself and therefore certainly won't be able to take care of her. The solution is for them to figure out what this visit really means to each of them and how committed they are to each other and to the relationship. Any relationship can survive if both partners are equally committed. Each fears being more committed than the other.

THE RESOLUTION

Both need to discuss what the differences in their life-style mean now and for any potential future, and they probably need to plan on hiring a cleaning person if they do decide they want to live together. The C word here is not "clean" but "commitment." When relationships change levels, communication is crucial. If a relationship has moved very quickly, the stages are less apparent, the trust is less well founded, the expectations loom even larger than they normally do, and communication is often less skilled just because the participants do not know each other very well. If an argument seems out of proportion to the event, it most likely centers on an unspoken concern. Figure out what both of you are *really* talking about.

Affection vs. Sex

♥

THE GAME

They have been hanging out at her house all day, watching the football game, doing chores, keeping busy. She is fixing dinner, and he comes up and puts his arm around her and begins snuggling and kissing the back of her neck. She playfully pushes him away, but when he becomes more insistent, she gets angry, and they're both off and running again about the fact that she's frigid and he's only after one thing.

THE BLAME

HE feels that she's uptight, really doesn't enjoy sex, and wants everything on her terms. He thinks she wants him to be able to perform only if and when she's ready, and on cue. He was just feeling loving and tender at that moment and wanted her to know it.

SHE thinks he's insensitive and forever horny. He never seems willing to be playful or friendly or fun or romantic, just horny, and even then, only when it's incredibly inconvenient is he at all interested in being sexy. It's his way of asserting control.

THE EXPLANATION

Neither men nor women are very good at differentiating sex and affection. Most men are affectionate mostly when they are feeling sexual, whereas women really like affection for its own sake—they like the feeling of being close and physical with no further expectations or obligations.

HE very likely *was* feeling affectionate rather than sexual, at least initially, but since he didn't say anything, she assumed that he was interested in some bedroom action from the very beginning, and she was busy. He interpreted her initial pleasure as encouragement, but then he started getting turned on, and the more excited and insistent he got, the less she was. So he began intensifying his efforts to see if he couldn't "convince" her, even though his original impulse was just affectionate. If he's being completely honest, he might even admit that after a frustrating few minutes, the whole thing became a battle of wills. Not very sexy and not much fun for either.

SHE feels that the only time he's ever turned on is when she's doing something for him, which makes it doubly demeaning. Not only is it completely centered on him and what he wants, but it's inconvenient. Just once, she would like to feel that she could get hugged without getting bedded. It always has to be his way on his terms, and if she says no, then he sulks. The whole thing makes her feel used and impersonal. And it's a battle of wills for her too.

THE RESOLUTION

Both he and she really want the same things: to feel appreciated and loved and cherished and in some degree of control. Words would go a long way toward at least clarifying some of the confusion. If when he's feeling snuggly, he would say, "You're such fun to be with, I just want to hug you," and she could take a moment to hug him back, a struggle would be less likely. Commenting on her physical attributes will not have the same effect, incidentally. In fact, quite the opposite, probably. If she said, "I've got time for a quick hug, but more fun stuff will have to wait until after dinner," he would not only not be hurt, but would have the fun of anticipation.

It also wouldn't hurt if she could see her way clear to take the initiative occasionally in both limited affection and lovemaking overtures. But it is as important for her to distinguish between the two as it is for him. On the face of it, it is impossible to distinguish affection from foreplay without verbalization. Intensity and duration are not useful differentiations until it's already too late. Both affection and sex are valuable components in any relationship, but it's important to be able to tell which is which and understand where they overlap.

Family
and Relatives

♥

THE GAME

Whenever he doesn't call, pulls one of his shenanigans, or otherwise disappoints her, her mom is always there with a cup of tea and a dose of sympathy. At family gatherings, she has noted a definite coolness on the family's part toward him, and even he has commented that they don't seem to like him much. Recently, they seem to be fighting more and more about her mother's attitude toward him, and she finds herself defending Mom and being angry at him. He feels caught in the middle, defensive, and just plain sad.

THE BLAME

HE doesn't understand why he's always wrong when it comes to her family. They certainly treat her like a second-class citizen, and while it's okay for her to complain, if he dares to say anything less than glowing, he gets it in the teeth.

SHE realizes that her family can be difficult, but his constant criticism makes her wonder if he's just making fun of her by complaining about her family. His family isn't exactly a bargain. They could go for months without seeing or talking to him.

THE EXPLANATION

SHE is mainly to blame in this situation on two separate counts. First, she complains about him to Mom, and then once the two of them have made up, Mom is still left the repository of the sadness and anger. She's not in on the kiss and make-up. So the bad taste lingers. Second, she's setting up the same thing in reverse by complaining about Mom to him, so he's left either trying to make peace, which is a thankless position, or defending her against Mom, which is great on a short-term basis but absolutely won't work on any long-term basis.

HE is less involved with his family and they are less involved with the relationship for several reasons. First, most men are less involved with their families once they leave home simply because men are encouraged to be more independent, unless they are the only male child and Dad is dead or otherwise out of the picture. Even then, most men feel mixed about staying in very close contact with Mom. Even when they are close, most don't fill Mom in on the graphic details of the relationship when things aren't going right, so his family has less ammunition against her than her family has to do him in. As is often the case, opposites attract in terms of family styles. Often individuals are as taken with a partner's family—either closeness or distance—as they are by the partner, and it seems preferable to the one in which they were raised. So there is almost always a radical difference in style.

THE RESOLUTION

If either partner views the relationship as having *any* long-term potential, neither partner must complain to the other about family nor to family about the partner. That's why acquaintances, diaries, and therapists were invented. Even acquaintances who may become friends are tricky here, since friends will remember the fights and hold the grudges long after the principles have mended their differences. Most people aren't that crazy about the way they were raised, but will defend family with tigerlike ferocity if it is attacked from outside.

An important corollary is that family should never complain to one partner about the other even in the service of trying to be supportive. Those nasty little comments have a way of being overheard, misunderstood, taken out of context, and *remembered*. It is comforting to complain when somebody has done somebody wrong, but the limits and hurt feelings live on in the sympathetic listener's mind and heart and will return to haunt the confessor.

Housework

♥

THE GAME

She delights in helping him clean up his place on the weekend and is perfectly willing to help out in the kitchen. At her place, however, she is the lone inhabitant of the kitchen while he's parked in front of the TV. He has never even offered to run the vacuum when she's hosting a party for his friends.

THE BLAME

HE doesn't really understand what the fuss is all about. He's never asked her to clean his place. She just seems to want it neater than he does. And as for the kitchen, he kind of likes to putter around on his own, but boy, should he even stir her sauce, she goes crazy. So it's easier to just keep out of the way.

SHE figures fair is fair. They both have places, both pay rent, and if she helps out at his place, he should help out at hers. She reasons he likes the idea of a liberated woman as long as that means that there's something in it for him. When it comes to dusting, he's a Neanderthal man.

THE EXPLANATION

The times they are a-changing, but they haven't hit the bathroom or kitchen yet. No matter how immaculate a house may be, women find themselves apologizing for its condition, and no matter how grungy it is, men never do. It seems to be a cultural assumption that the only truly neat men are gay. Women tend to see themselves as comfortably domestic, or at least their neatness is no threat to their femininity; this is definitely not the case for men. A man in an apron is not considered a sex symbol.

THE RESOLUTION

SHE doesn't have to clean his house or help cook food at his house. If his house is his responsibility and meals on his turf are either ordered in or defrosted, she may find that while her stomach suffers, the relationship doesn't. If she finds his house too disgusting for human habitation, she can calmly and gently explain why they're spending more time on her neatly vacuumed turf. At her house, the converse is true. She's responsible, and since she's not offering to help at his pigsty, she shouldn't feel he has to help at hers. Of course, if they decide to cohabit, the issue is a bit more complex. If only one works outside the home, the homebody gets the homework, not on the basis of sexual destiny, but because the one who's home is there and the one who works outside brings outside stuff in and it just makes sense. Huge chores need to be decided on and divided up, but asking the person who's been out working all day to come home and work isn't fair. If both work outside, eat out, and hire someone to clean if possible, or draw straws for tasks, or each choose what he or she hates doing least and then bid on the truly terrible tasks. Fair is fair, not political.

Competition

♥

THE GAME

They're having their first dinner party since they've been an item. He's decided to pitch in and surprise her. He's taken the afternoon off from work, let himself into her apartment, scoured the bathroom, and taken a quick pass with the vacuum, and he has started on the salad when she comes in. He expects to win the Boyfriend of the Year award and instead finds her a bit cold and distant throughout the evening. Admittedly she did say thank you, but he accurately felt that her heart wasn't in it. He is crestfallen, to say the least, and decides never again to lend a hand.

THE BLAME

HE feels that he was just trying to help out and be a good guy. He knows how important it is to her to make a good impression, and he's not exactly sure what went wrong.

SHE feels like a real jerk. She knows he was just trying to help out and she's not sure why she's feeling upset, but she sure is. It's not as if he's so all-fired helpful around the house ordinarily. It's almost as though he's trying to show her up in front of company.

THE EXPLANATION

With more and more women working outside of the home, the traditional roles for men and women have been altered, perhaps irrevocably. The fact that many women make as much if not more money, have equally important and satisfying careers, and work as long hours as men hasn't helped matters at all. Everybody needs to feel he or she has something unique and important to contribute not only to society but to the relationship. When the role distinctions get blurred, individual areas of expertise become even more significant.

He may legitimately have been trying to help out, or he may have been trying to put her in her place a bit. (Ha—if you can do what I can do, I can do what you can do.)

She may have felt some genuine gratitude, but it was overshadowed by her need to feel feminine and domestic. She may not have realized this need until she came home and found him in her apron, in her kitchen. It may be difficult for her to admit such a need. But admit it she must.

THE RESOLUTION

In the most perfect of all worlds, there would be no competition, merely cooperation, play, and pleasure in accomplishment—either our own or another's. But the world isn't perfect, and sex roles are in transition, so the basic rule for nonhostile intimate relationships is to be where your partner's not.

If he's good at cars, she can cook, or even vice versa. If she likes cooking, it's not that he can't help out, but he should ask first and admit that he's only puttering around, not trying to match her real skill. If he's good at talking, you can be good at drawing. This isn't a plea for a return to role-playing or games between men and women but a simple acknowledgment that competition isn't all that useful in intimate relationships, because by definition, somebody has to win and somebody has to lose. Separate but equal divisions of labor and expertise with occasional permitted forays into the other's territory will ensure a longer and happier basis than constant competition. Only the habitual winner will tell you that competition is healthy. It doesn't feel that way to the perpetual loser. Even if the "teams" are evenly matched, an unnecessary note of tension and scorekeeping is introduced.

If he wants to help out on her turf, he should ask first, and perhaps when it's not public and only if he is willing to allow her to make forays into his important areas. (Clue: important areas aren't always sexually determined. Anytime somebody wants to cook or clean in my house, come along. On the other hand, I'm not terribly interested in your psychological assessment of my last chapter.)

Part of the anguish here might have been avoided had he chosen to do something "special" for the party such as buy flowers or provide a special dessert, but even here, a discussion of what was expected, while less romantic, might have secured domestic tranquillity.

Bitching

♥

THE GAME

They have had a terrible argument. Some measure of peace has been restored. They have both apologized; they have made love and promised never to let such a trivial issue part them again. They are both just nodding off to sleep when she mentions the matter under dispute. He cannot believe it and pretends he's already asleep. She is resolute, at first kiddingly, then more urgently, until he finally turns to her and says, "Look, let's forget about it. It's over." She says okay and then starts up again. He jumps out of bed, pulls on his pants and a T-shirt, and slams out the door, hollering that he's going for a walk.

THE BLAME

HE figured it was over and done with. They'd chewed it to death. He's apologized, so enough already. He has never gotten over her ability to regurgitate past unhappinesses. Why not leave it alone and get on with whatever is around the corner? Rehashing a baseball game is one thing—that's pleasurable, not an argument. Her incessant "you said, I said" makes him absolutely crazy.

. . .

SHE has the sense that he will say anything to end an argument. He doesn't mean it, won't live by it, or most likely even remember it, and she's tired of having the same stuff come up over and over again. If it doesn't get solved this time, they'll just be fighting over it again soon. He calls her a nag, but she just wants things to be smooth and happy between them, and talking about it is the only way she knows to figure out what went wrong this time, what each of them thought was going on, and how to fix it.

THE EXPLANATION

Men are not crazy about going back over defeats, and if unpleasant memories are tied in with issues they either don't understand or can't control, so much more reason to forget them. By and large in the male world, results are what count, pathways are less significant, and what's done is done. After an argument it's time to move on, lick wounds if necessary, but get on with it, girding up for the next battle.

Women, sometimes less conversant with power issues, are often intrigued with the underpinings. If you don't have control, you're much more likely to be interested in subtleties and means. Women are also much more used to dealing with emotions, so the content of the discussion is less threatening to them.

THE RESOLUTION

While it is true that men can recite baseball scores and statistics for players who died before they were born, emotional amnesia allows them to function in circumstances in which they feel inept and incompetent. This doesn't mean that no discussion of the past is allowed, but it means that any discussion best have a specific point other than his admitting that he blew it one more time. If it's a rehash for the sake of going back and picking through the ashes, both parties are best served by letting it go.

If she thinks a point has been overlooked, it should be specifically cited before the final resolution, apology, and lovemaking take place. In his mind, that signals the end of the dispute. The "you always, you nevers" add very little new information and a lot of heat to arguments.

Instead of walking or rather storming out, he might have pointed out what further point could be gleaned from all this, and she might have had her own point ready, rather than sneaking up on it. Her timing also leaves a lot to be desired. Once a truce is called or a treaty established, no fair going back over the conflict. It is useless and inflammatory and makes him feel that nothing is ever resolved, that no matter what he does it's never enough.

Opinions

♥

THE GAME

They are planning a party together. She is trying to figure out which of his friends he wants to invite, what to serve, whether to have an open bar or make do with wine and beer, whether to make it an evening or afternoon party, and what to wear. When she tries to talk with him about it, he keeps saying, "Whatever you decide is fine with me, dear." She is furious. Not only does he not seem to care, but she is sure that he will criticize her if anything isn't absolutely perfect.

THE BLAME

HE first of all doesn't really care about the party at all. Second, he knows that she is much better at giving parties than he is and she will only make fun of his suggestions anyway. What does he know about giving a party? Throw a couple of steaks on the barby and keep the beer cold and coming. She won't take no for an answer, but she acts as though she thinks he's an uncultured lout if he offers an opinion. Heads she wins, tails he loses.

· · ·

SHE is doing this for him as much as for herself. The least he can do is show a little interest and help her out a bit. If she makes it too fancy, he'll accuse her of trying to make him look clumsy, and he's always complaining that she doesn't take his feelings into account.

THE EXPLANATION

Both men and women are constantly accusing the other of not having an opinion on the important stuff. It's just that they disagree about what's important, and herein lies the problem. Men feel that women don't ever have an opinion when they ask, "What do you want to do tonight? Where would you like to go? What movie would you like to see?" "I'll be happy with whatever you decide" isn't very helpful, especially when he feels that she really does have an opinion and is just unwilling to express it now, but boy, will he hear about it later. She feels much the same about his attitude toward her clothes or her friends or what to buy his mother for her birthday. In both situations, the person seeking the opinion views the matter as more important than the person refusing to state an opinion. The nonresponsive party not only doesn't care as much, but often feels at a disadvantage in terms of knowledge, power, expertise, and control.

A woman has been conditioned to defer to the man's choice of outing, and the geisha tradition is viewed as part of ensnaring a man. Be compliant, be easy to get along with, do it his way, stroke his ego. Thus lies the path of femininity as well as permanence. The fact that he is most likely going to pay for dinner also encourages her to leave the decision-making to him. Most women feel that if they choose the wrong restaurant and the food is expensive or lousy, they lose points and will be viewed as grasping, incompatible, or difficult to get along with.

Men feel similar sentiments about offering opinions in areas which they have very little knowledge or experience. Opinions concerning her clothing they often quickly learn to keep to themselves when they criticize her favorite new dress and are told they know nothing about fashion or style or what looks good and if they're so smart how come they always wear that striped shirt with that brown suit. Men until very recently had a limited number of choices, and potential mistakes, to make in their own wardrobes and often feel at a disadvantage helping her deal with hers.

Underlying any squeamishness about decision-making is the risk of saying the wrong thing, of making a mistake. The earlier in the relationship the opinion is solicited, the more problematic it's going to be. Neither knows much about the other, and each is trying to put the best foot forward. Both are still eagerly committed to fostering the impression that the two are indeed soulmates and effortlessly agree on everything.

THE RESOLUTION

If the real problem is risk-taking, not vacuousness—that is, if both partners *have* opinions but are just reluctant to express them—then the solution lies in reducing the risk factor. This can be done by both people realizing that differences in opinion are not necessarily lethal, and if they are frequent in the relationship they will either both learn to tolerate them early on or the relationship will not survive. So the problem is not in having opinions, but in expressing them. The following rules can at least diminish the problem: (1) If you have an opinion and are asked for it, express it calmly, quickly and succinctly. (2) If the subject is something you care little about, share that feeling, but also share a preference. (3) If you care a lot about the subject, share that feeling as well as an opinion. (4) Be willing to have your opinion ignored. (5) Be willing to state that you are getting tired of having your opinion continually ignored and you would prefer not to be queried if you're not going to be heeded. (6) Be gentle in your disagreement with and opinion about the other person's opinions.

Trying constantly to please the other person at the expense of your own sense of self is hard not only on you, but on your partner as well. We are our opinions, and trying to play good little kid to our partner's huge and potentially angry parent is a time bomb.

Let's Just Be Friends

♥

THE GAME

They had once been lovers and have kept up a long-distance relationship consisting of phone calls, off-color birthday cards, sentimental Christmas cards, and occasional visits. He was a frequent flier and announced he wanted to pay her a visit. As his pay-off for losing a Super-Bowl bet to her he offered to buy her a fancy dinner if she would put him up in her back bedroom. She was not completely stupid, so was sure to clarify her position that she was not interested in a drop-in lover, but looked forward to seeing him as long as he understood that she was willing to be a friend and nothing more. He arrived, promptly began massaging her neck, and was miffed when she reminded him of their "deal."

THE BLAME

SHE is furious that he could pull such a cheap trick after she had overcome her embarrassment and gone to all of the trouble of making everything perfectly clear before he came. Granted, he was the one making the effort to come and visit, but she feels that providing a place for him to stay is a fair discharge of her part of their deal.

HE can't believe that she is being such a tease or at least a poor sport. He didn't come all that way to sight-see, and besides, what did she expect once they were under the same roof? She would probably be just as angry if he *hadn't* made a pass.

THE EXPLANATION

He and she view friendship and back bedrooms quite differently. She has a number of platonic male friends, although admittedly, most are either involved or gay. She would never think of making overtures to any of her women friends' men, so she has a number of precedents for her belief that platonic friendships between men and women are possible. Besides, she figured it would be kind of fun to have some of the electricity around without having to act anything out.

He, like most men, isn't all that experienced with platonic friendships and somehow figures he is exercising his male prerogative as well as responsibility and that he is expected as a self-respecting male to make a pass at any faintly eligible woman for chivalry's sake if nothing else. Besides, they once had something going, and she obviously was warm and comfortable with him, so what's to lose?

THE RESOLUTION

Men are simply not as experienced at the subtleties of friendship as women. Her actions belied her words to him because he simply has no experience with the concept that she is espousing. He confuses her affection with sexual accessibility and feels betrayed by her rejection of his pass.

Their situation just has too much history to be completely without sexual content for either. One of the ways to teach a new lesson is with constant, gentle reinforcement along the way. Few complicated lessons are learned in one session, especially when they go counter to conventional sexual wisdom and custom.

Most men have been taught to think of sex as control and masculinity. In an ambiguous situation, it is not unusual for either or both parties to try to exert some control by doing what they know best. She is offering the familiar comfort of friendship, he is asserting his masculinity via seduction. Difficult lessons are often most easily learned on neutral turf, if for no other reason than lack of confusing associations. She probably would have been much better able to make her point if he had been staying in a hotel or if she arranged for him to stay with a male friend. (The same scenario would likely have been played out if she agreed to stay with him on a visit.)

Talk can only go so far if all the other cues seem to be shouting contradictory information. If she doesn't intend to let him into her bed, it's probably not a great idea to let him into her house, unless she's willing to have him at least make a try for the sheets. Then she can't plead total innocence.

Loneliness

THE GAME

He has been separated for three months and living in a furnished sublet. She has been divorced for four years. They have whirlwinded each other, seeing each other every night since they met at a singles' dance. Because they have spent so much time together for the last six weeks, it seemed perfectly logical to talk about his moving in, which he did after four weeks. Now, three months later, everything seems to be unraveling, and neither can figure out exactly why.

THE BLAME

SHE was initially ecstatic: finally, a man able to commit. She never doubted for a moment that they could make it together, since he was willing to move in. Now he seems like a completely different guy. The romance is gone, the sex is infrequent and indifferent, and she feels much more like a wife than a lover. She knows about the risks of being a transitional woman, since he has been separated for such a short period of time, and she knows it would be wise to let some time go by, but there are so few good ones around that she figures she should grab 'em while they're hot or somebody else will.

. . .

HE is a bit mystified about their problems as well. She was delightful during their brief dating period but seems to have gotten possessive and jealous and turned into someone who bears resemblance to a prison warden or his mother, or worst of all, his ex-wife. If he'd wanted to be married, he could have stayed with Ms. Alimony.

THE EXPLANATION

SHE views living together as marriage with training wheels. It's just a modern, kind of hip way of saying that in a little while we'll get around to doing it officially, but it's all done but the ministerial shouting and will be official when his divorce becomes final. Admittedly, she was flattered and relieved when he committed to her, since she's old-fashioned enough to be concerned that he might just move on when he got tired of the sex, and this way she knows that he genuinely loves and cares about and is committed to her. She knows she's sold on him, and living together certainly has taken the worry out of being close. She assumes that living together is a commitment for him because it is a commitment for her. Why else would he suggest moving in?

While she's not crazy about not having a man around, her home has always been a warm, comfortable respite from the crazy outside world. She has filled it with her things, tastes, friends, and smells, although she is perfectly willing to clean out a bureau for him and move some of her clothes into storage so he can have half the closet.

HE hates living alone. A new bed, a new woman, not knowing where his socks or his car or his keys are in the morning—it's all a drag. He loves the security of a familiar nest, and the fact that she is a warm and loving woman is an added advantage. If he really looked closely at his own motives, he would find that a large part of the appeal of this relationship is the living together, not the intimacy or the sex but the familiar surroundings, a comfortable place to return to after work. Cooking for himself, cleaning up, coming home to an empty house with only a TV for company make him feel old and used-up and tired.

THE RESOLUTION

There are lots of warning signs here. He's too newly out of a relationship, she's not terribly comfortable about her sexuality outside of marriage (or at least a trial marriage) but feels that if she doesn't act immediately, he'll disappear. But the root trouble is that she views living together as a step that inevitably leads to marriage, and he views it as a welcome alternative to a dreary bachelor pad. Neither is purposely misleading the other, but each is a bit shy about admitting that sometimes, the ancient stereotypes hold true. She's the nest builder and he likes having a warm, dry familiar cave to which to return at day's end.

Admitting up front what a domestic arrangement means to both, commitment to one and convenience to the other, might be initially painful, but it also might have avoided the current bewildered unpleasantness. They might have been able to compromise on a couple of nights at her house, a couple of nights at his, and a couple of nights alone. That way they would have been able to learn each other's style, allow the process of discovery to unfold a bit more slowly. He could decide whether he likes her or her decor. She could be honest about her need for commitment or at least her view of where their relationship might lead rather than assuming that they're on the same track.

Of course, allowing him more time to be single makes sense, but relationships aren't always sensible. Still, dealing with underlying, basic, tightly held convictions and assumptions at least gives impetuousity a firm base on which to exist.

In this case, she must acknowledge that his unwillingness to be alone isn't the same as being committed to her, and he needs to deal with her fears about being sexually used without some form of commitment from him and understand that living together is a larger commitment to her than it is to him.

The Anniversary Test

♥

THE GAME

The anniversary of their first kiss is coming up. She breathlessly awaits the day, sure he too will remember, because this relationship is so much deeper and he is much more sensitive than any other guy she has dated. When he doesn't mention it in advance, she assumes he's planning a surprise, which makes her breathless and giggly with anticipation. She has his gift all ready and can hardly wait to see his face. She decides to go first, prolonging her own suspense even longer. She valiantly tries to hide the tears and disappointment once it has become abundantly clear that he has no surprise, no gift, literally no remembrance.

THE BLAME

HE feels like a complete jerk, but good heavens, their first *kiss*. His mom was always carping about his dad forgetting anniversaries, but this is ridiculous. She's acting like a little girl. There's a real world out there—how the hell is he supposed to remember all this trash? There's something to commemorate almost every day.

. . .

SHE was absolutely sure that he would remember, that she meant as much to him as he to her. She was so sure that she had at last found a soulmate, and now she feels disappointed, stupid, angry, and unsure whether she should go on with this entanglement at all.

THE EXPLANATION

She is testing him perhaps without even being aware that she is doing so. She is comparing him with every other guy she has ever dated and hoping he measures up to the thoughtful ones (who have failed her on some other level) and beats out the beasts who have the sensitivity of aardvarks in heat. And the former love she is really holding him up to for comparison is her first true love. Yep . . . Dad. She is playing little girl on Christmas morning believing that her heart's desire will be fulfilled by the big guy (regardless of the fact that Mom probably did the shopping anyway). Even if Dad was or is an insensitive clod, to a little girl there is always hope that this time he will come through. This set of expectations has been transferred to the current man in her life, and what it boils down to is one big test.

Inevitably, sooner or later, he will disappoint her, because—surprise—he's not Dad, and more important, she's not five years old anymore.

Daddy may love you no matter how hard you push him, and sometimes pushing is even kind of fun, but it's a disastrous pattern once puberty is attained, because it is doomed.

THE RESOLUTION

On the simplest level, if it's important to her she might tell him ahead of time. They can discuss it and decide what to do. He's not a lout if he remembers different things (his high school batting average) from the ones she does. Part of the exploration process in a relationship is discerning what's important to the other person and why. Some surprises are fun, but if you *know* it's important to you, clue the other person in.

On a much more complicated level, testing is dangerous, doomed behavior, since nobody can measure up to the stature a parent has in a five-year-old's mind. The trick is to get past the kindergarten mentality. Daddy may be pushable because deep down we know he's bigger, stronger, and wiser and will love us no matter what we do. The same rules simply don't apply when we're talking about grown-up relationships. Cute is pretty much a no-no if a sane, stable interaction is what's desired. The desires of our hearts must be communicated when known and searched for when unclear. They should not be laid at the feet of a lover who is supposed to read minds (as in "If you loved me, you'd know").

Security

♥

THE GAME

They have been dating for nearly a year and living together for six months. They plan to marry when it is mutually convenient. What was once a bawdy, passionate sex life has become nearly nonexistent. He says he loves her, but he's tired and distracted by work. She is frantically trying to figure out whether there's someone else or he has gotten tired of her already.

THE BLAME

HE sees her as being hopelessly romantic when it comes to sex and love. He isn't fooling around—he's just a bit busy and distracted. Her constant nagging and worrying and begging for reassurance is making him crazy. He has told her that he loves her, and if that should ever change, he'll tell her that too.

SHE is terrified. He used to be charming and couldn't wait to get her into bed, and now he acts as though she's got bad breath or something. She's tried ignoring the problem, talking with him about it, teasing him, and goading him, but nothing seems to work. She's trying to decide whether she should move out, have an affair, or just get used to having a platonic lover.

THE EXPLANATION

HE has been conditioned to think of the chase as the important part of courtship: seduction, bribery. It is his biological responsibility to bed his choice and convince her that he's the best she can do. Once that challenge has been met and he's won her, he figures he can relax and get back to some of the things he's been neglecting, like work and friends and sports and his mom. It's not that he loves her any less, but he devoted an awful lot of time and money and effort to wooing her, and he's happy he did, but now it's back to business as usual, literally.

SHE, unfortunately, has been conditioned in a diametrically opposite way. Once she believed that he really loved her and cherished her above all others and was really turned on by her, she thought she could afford to be a little less reticent about a whole lot of things, including sex. She feels more open to him since he has proved to her that he cared, that he wasn't just after one thing and then planning to abandon her. It seems just as she's really getting comfortable about and interested in sex, he's tuning out and turning off.

THE RESOLUTION

Both he and she need to realize that relationships are ever-changing, and even though society may dictate a rather rigid and outdated set of expectations about male and female behavior, each of them can use those modern brains to see through the obvious limitations.

Men, it is not enough to tell her you love her and then assume that takes care of the issue forever, any more than it makes sense to tell a secretary that she's doing a good job and then say nothing more until she makes a mistake. An employee needs more feedback from a boss, and people in our lives need feedback too.

On the other hand, assuming that the primary responsibilities for courtship will be his for ever and ever is unrealistic and exploitative. If women want to be treated as equals, it makes some sense for them to take at least some of the responsibility for making sure that a relationship stays fresh and sexy and new, including taking some sexual initiative and not settling into a physical, emotional, or sexual complacency. The societal markings are old and deep, but they can be modified and freshened so that both he and she feel loved and lovable.

Intimacy and Insecurity

♥

THE GAME

They have been dating exclusively for three months. They are both grown-ups and have a difficult time with commitment, communication, and trust. So what's new? He has to be out of town for a couple of days on business, but promises to call. It has now been two days and she hasn't heard from him. She decides he's played her for a fool and vows never to trust him again, and when he finally does call on the third day she is barely civil. He asks if anything is wrong and she says, "Nothing."

THE BLAME

HE really meant to call her earlier, but his plane was late and he was tired the first night, and the second night he was out with a client and started to excuse himself to call her, but he'd had a bit too much to drink and the guys started ribbing him about having to check in and he began to feel a bit foolish, and now, when he finally gets a minute, she's causing icicles to form on his earlobe. He was feeling a bit apologetic about not calling earlier, but now views her as demanding. It's not as if he were on holiday. It is business, after all.

SHE sees this as proof that he really isn't committed to the relationship and that he has forgotten about her when he's away. He seems childish and petulant. After all, he said he would call, and he knows how much she looks forward to hearing from him and how much she misses him when he's gone. He's probably glad to be away from her and their somewhat domesticized situation and clearly is unready to settle down and treat this relationship as worthy of respect. And if he doesn't respect the relationship, he obviously doesn't respect her.

THE EXPLANATION

If this game seems remarkably similar to the initial stages of courtship where she is sitting around waiting for the phone to ring and he loses his nerve after too long a period of time has gone by, you're paying attention. And something is definitely wrong. After three months, a relationship should not bear a whole lot of resemblance to the early, uncertain, awkward beginning moves of the game. Either this relationship has not really taken hold, or another stage is being approached, or most painfully, there is a bit of both.

Both he and she are having some difficulty with commitment. She is asking for constant reassurance, he wants to feel that he doesn't have to reassure her constantly. This tug-of-war is as old as the myth that women entrap and men try to escape. She views his unwillingness to keep in touch as a statement that he really doesn't love her after all. He views her iciness as petty and selfish. He's tired, he's working but he wanted to check in with her for a few minutes, talk sexy, and know that she was looking forward to his return the next day. He sees her as a distraction to his work, and admitting that he misses her seems wimpy, unmanly, and dangerous, since he really needs to concentrate on his job.

For most men, work is still the primary function and definition of life. Relationships are important, but by nature they must be secondary, since no reasonable woman would want a bum or a loser.

To most women, a career is fine, but a relationship with a good man is what makes the world go around. She can juggle her work and still be there for him, so why can't he? Difference in conditioning, priorities, and experience is part of the answer.

And that's just the easy part. Since both men and women in this society are raised by women, little girls form an identity with their moms as the same-sex parent and it is not until adolescence or later that independence becomes a factor, at least in terms of sexual identity. A little boy has to separate much earlier if he is to form a separate sexual identity. Feeling too close, too intimate, with Mom threatens his sense of himself as masculine, which can be painfully echoed in his adult life. This may become a problem if either his sexual identity is weak or threatened or if he becomes involved with a woman like Mom (and Freud maintains it's the only way to go) or one who is powerful or nurturing and desirous of intimacy.

THE RESOLUTION

HE has to understand that he is not less manly for feeling lonesome or incomplete when she isn't with him. Intimacy can be habit-forming, and it doesn't make either of them less sovereign if he is more involved and happier when she is around. He has to realize that even John Wayne wasn't always hanging out with his horse or the boys. Softness isn't contagious, and because she is soft doesn't mean he will become so.

SHE has to stop assuming that she is unlovable. It makes her think that whenever he makes a mistake or doesn't do what she wants or expects him to do, he has just proved that he really doesn't value her. If she believes she is lovable and if in fact he loves her, as he continually demonstrates, whether he calls her today or tomorrow is only interesting, not threatening. He cannot prove that she is lovable. She has to believe that herself or she will constantly be asking him for a suffocating reassurance that neither he nor anyone else can provide. Relationships can enhance our self-esteem or undermine it. But they cannot provide it, and if we let a relationship destroy it, we are damn fools.

Both he and she need to believe that they are loved and decide how better to ask for specific reassurances without constantly acting out their own uncertainties. Growing up in America means growing up insecure, but at some point, we do grow up and take responsibility for our own lovability. Once he believes she loves him, her wish to speak to him is endearing, not entrapping. Once she believes she is lovable, whether he calls tonight or tomorrow is of only minor importance.

As for the deeper and more complicated issues of her independence and his ability to tolerate closeness without claustrophobia or the compromising of his sexual identity, both must be aware of the problem before it can be tackled. It is very likely something that has bedeviled both of their relationships for many years and will continue to do so until either she finds a man with a completely unthreatenable sexual identity, he finds a less nurturing woman who reminds him less of his mother, or they both find a good therapist and begin to do some work. It would make adult sexuality a great deal simpler if children were raised by both mothers and fathers rather than so one-sidedly by moms. (Substituting dads for moms won't work. There needs to be a balance: one for nurturing, one for accomplishment.)

Sex in the Morning

♥

THE GAME

He wakes up amorous, and while she's still asleep he's on top of her, trying to kiss her and turn her on. She's pouty and turned off and insulted, because she figures anybody would have done for him just then. She's not even awake, so how much can his ardor have to do with her?

THE BLAME

HE feels she wants to have sex only when it's convenient for her, when she's had a drink or two or when she's just out of the shower or just gotten home from a party. He's tired at night, but starting the day off with a little loving seems a terrific idea as far as he's concerned, and he's getting sick of her selfishness.

SHE feels disconnected from him. She's definitely not a morning person and figures it's only going to be slam-bam, thank you ma'am, since both of them have to get to work. He's never tender in the morning and concentrates more on his own pleasure than on hers, and it's so gross and animalistic—no romance whatsoever. She also figures that if he thinks about making love all day, as she now will, he'll be really ready by tonight and it will be that much better for both of them.

THE EXPLANATION

For many men, early-morning sex seems logical and straightforward for a number of reasons. First, most men experience early-morning erections anyway which are a combination of a full bladder, a good night's sleep, and perhaps even a leftover dream or two. Given male anatomy, getting ready for sex is either significantly easier or harder than it is for a woman. Once a male's body is ready, his mind can be made to follow—approximately the opposite of the way it works for a female. It is partly this reality that makes her think that he's not really interested in her, but just in her body.

For a lot of men, wasting a nice erection is a shameful thing. Besides, dealing again with straight biology, the very factors that make a woman feel romantic—a long fun evening together, being a little tipsy and perhaps a bit tired—are not very helpful or conducive to an erect penis. She's ready at night partly because her traditional sexual posture is one of relative passivity, whereas his biological destiny is by anatomy more aggressive. A good night's sleep can be a tremendous help.

Neither has really addressed another basic issue here, beyond anatomy, and that has to do with smells. Women live in constant fear of offending somebody's nose. Most are concerned that without constant washing, perfuming, or hiding, most of their orifices will emit yucky odors.

Even those women who accept their own sweat as being normal (thank goodness for aerobics) are secretly convinced that their mouths harbor unthinkable stenches which would be repugnant and a total turn-off. They are not thrilled with the idea of smelling a partner's breath either, but the basic concern is still for their own odors. Which is probably also at least partly why women are mystified by men's interest in performing oral sex. Men are much more comfortable with what women often classify as unpleasant odors. But then, early on, men treat burping and farting as fun things to practice. Sweat is considered manly and honest. It took Joe Namath to convince men it was okay to shower and use aftershave and deodorant.

Even as we approach the end of the twentieth century, women still clutch the idea of romance firmly to their well-developed pectorals. This romanticism also favors longer, hazier sex, which usually favors evening rather than early-morning sex.

THE RESOLUTION

Both he and she need to talk about what sex means to and for each of them. Every meal doesn't have to be a gourmet extravaganza, and every sexual experience doesn't have to take four hours. There is a place in everybody's life for some occasional fast food. If she could be certain (1) that he really was thinking of her, even early in the morning, (2) that he would be responsible for making coffee so she could get into the bathroom first, (3) that he would set his alarm a half hour earlier in case he woke up feeling amorous, (4) that he would also be willing to indulge in more romantic encounters, (5) that he truly doesn't mind morning breath, (6) that it might pay to be honest about other bodily smells of hers as well as his, then she might (1) understand that a little variety in their sex life makes sense, (2) be willing to approach him when she's feeling romantic at night and not necessarily wait for him to make the first move when he's feeling sexy, (3) be honest about her own misgivings about the way she looks and smells and feels, (4) decide how much romance is fun and how much is a snare that makes him feel he's playing a part that has nothing to do with his own personality or wants or needs. Then the two of them might find that they really are crazy about each other rather than just crazy. Taking turns about initiating sex and choosing the time and style might be terrific for both.

Impotence

♥

THE GAME

They have been to a party, and both have had a bit too much to drink. The dancing was fun and the flirting with strangers as well as each other made them very eager to get home and consummate their passion. Unfortunately, his spirit was willing but his body refused to cooperate. She was understanding and encouraging, but the next morning, the same thing happened. They are now at the point where they make sure that they go to bed at different times. He seems to think nothing is wrong. She is wondering whether he's having an affair.

THE BLAME

HE figures if she would just lose a bit of weight or stop being so aggressive or stop putting him down in public or if work just eased off a bit everything would be okay.

SHE is convinced that he really doesn't love her anymore, and she therefore is either going to have an affair, shame him into having sex with her, or turn him on so bad he can't help himself.

THE EXPLANATION

Undoubtedly one of the reasons that sex has historically been viewed as male prerogative is that if he is in charge, he can check out his equipment before he decides whether he is interested. As long as she can be considered to be doing him a favor rather than having any real sexual desire of her own, impotence is only a problem for him; she can be relieved of her duty and he can sort it out in time. Once he feels duty-bound to satisfy her, or even worse, once she approaches him wanting sex, the pressure is really on, and whatever the initial cause of his impotence, a psychological performance anxiety is the last thing he needs. The pressure he is placing on himself is difficult enough. The pressure from her can be overwhelming (especially if it's something he would have highly cherished in his more potent days). His inability to have or maintain an erection can be misinterpreted unless both are willing to be honest about their feelings and desires in a nonthreatening way.

THE RESOLUTION

If he can say, "Honey, I don't know what's wrong with me, but if you'll give me a little time and a bit of patience and let me get some sleep and let me be in charge of our sex life for a few days, maybe I can figure out what's wrong. I don't love anybody else, and you still turn me on. It's just that the combination of alcohol and exhaustion clobbered me once, and now all I do is worry about whether you still think I'm a real man, and worrying about it is the worst thing for it and me and our sex life. I will see my doctor to make sure it's not diabetes or some medication I'm taking, but I would appreciate your patience. In the meantime, maybe we can still snuggle and hug and kiss."

If she can lose weight because she'd feel happy about herself or buy some new underwear because it would be fun and not as a last-ditch attempt to turn him on, then she may be able to find some comfort in her own self-confidence and get off his back. Paradoxically, an occasion of impotence is one of the few times when her taking the initiative is likely to cause more harm than good, if he sees it as just one more example of her lack of respect for him and his male role, not to mention other male things.

In most cases, impotence is psychological and is not a symptom of infidelity or sexual boredom. It needs to be treated like any other temporary, embarrassing social or sexual problem. To take it personally is to miss the point. If she can trust her relationship and her man, assuming no other signals exist for not doing so, being gentle, patient, and understanding may mean that sex can come back better, richer, and fuller than ever.

Talking

THE GAME

He and she have been to a party at her boss's house. He has stayed by her side throughout the evening, unwilling to circulate and be his usual charming self. In the car going home, she sulks, he sits mutely. The next morning in bed, they make love, after which she turns to him and says, "We've got to talk." He says, "About what?" She storms out of the bedroom and out of the house.

THE BLAME

HE thinks she is acting like a looney tune. They were feeling relaxed and happy, and she has obviously recovered from her nervousness about the party at her boss's house. He was looking forward to some Sunday-morning peace and quiet and is perfectly willing to listen to her talk about almost anything. He was just curious about this morning's topic. He decides she's still worried about work or must be premenstrual or crazy.

SHE is tired of being the mother to his stupid child. He knows he acted like a fool last night, and the least he can do is apologize. He's always trying to finesse her and pretend everything is okay when it's obviously not. She was trying to be reasonable by doing things his way, not discussing things when they were both tired last night and waiting until after they reaffirmed that they really do care about each other this morning by making love, but now it's time to get to her agenda, and for him to play dumb is just plain unfair, condescending, and insulting.

THE EXPLANATION

Men and women treat talk very differently. They talk about different things to one another and among themselves. Women have been talking to one another since the cradle, and feelings are their coin of the realm. When there is something going wrong in a relationship, women want to talk it out, also when frightened, upset, overwhelmed, underwhelmed, or even happy. As far as women are concerned, talking is how a problem is solved. When a woman says, "Let's talk," most men cringe.

For most men, talking has to do with work or baseball. Problems are worked out by thinking, not talking. Feelings are usually something to be avoided. What is needed is logic and facts. Most men either aren't aware of or very comfortable with their feelings about personal issues, and as a result they feel that they're in alien territory when forced to think about—let alone talk about—such things.

For a man to communicate these awkward thoughts via unfamiliar words to an angry female who he is certain is trying to win is the stuff of which nightmares are made. He is certain that he, in losing, will have to do or admit to some incredibly humiliating thing. He's not very experienced, he's not very comfortable. He knows he's not very good at it and he's already feeling guilty and that he did something wrong to boot. He's thinking, "She wants something from me and since I'm not very good at this, I'm going to lose something." Thus, for a man, talking about feelings means getting nailed. Not much incentive for a man to sit down and talk things out.

That doesn't mean a woman can't talk or even convince a man to talk to her, but it does mean if a woman wants to be effective, not to mention fair, she has to understand where he's coming from and figure out a way to make him comfortable. The first step on the path is to make sure, lady, that you're listening, really listening, as opposed to merely using this whole "talk" exercise as an opportunity to criticize. More succinctly, if talk becomes a synonym for bitch, your communication days are numbered.

THE RESOLUTION

If men and women are ever to discuss "emotional stuff" together comfortably and profitably, men have to develop some skill and confidence in talking about feelings, and women have to stop using talking as a synonym for complaining. She can ask questions about work and really listen to what he's saying rather than tending to cooking or letting her eyes roll back in her head or interrupting or focusing on office gossip. It might not even be such a bad idea to learn about baseball.

When she does want to discuss complaints, a specific time for a gripe session can be booked with a specific agenda, a limited number of concerns that are precise and fewer in number than the partners' combined IQs. As long as the session is going to focus on problems, it makes some practical as well as emotional sense to acknowledge the things that are going well, the pleasures as well as the pain and irritation of living together.

He can allow himself to enter the twentieth century where men are allowed to be full human beings and have concerns, fears, gripes, and honest-to-goodness thoughts about "softer" stuff. Men, too, are entitled to feelings. One of the reasons men are so unfamiliar with them is that women have demanded that men shoulder most if not all of the responsibility for finances and decision making and always be strong and sure. There's not much room to express uncertainty or fear or doubt in that scenario. If women are going to ask men to talk, they have to be willing to hear what men are going to say, like it or not. If a gripe session is in order, make sure that the concern is specific and recent. Statements like "You always" or "You never" are inaccurate and counterproductive. Saying, "I felt like I was a possession last night at my boss's house. Next time I would prefer you mingling a bit," is much more productive than saying "Who do you think you are?" "I know you were being supportive last night, but you're so good at mixing, I would have loved being able to show you off" is even more productive. Being specific rather than philosophical—making specific suggestions for change—means that talking may be less anxiety-provoking and a lot more productive for both of you.

Birthdays

♥

THE GAME

She is eagerly looking forward to the first birthday of hers she will celebrate with him. She has been dropping casual hints for weeks, deliciously anticipating ever more romantic scenarios. Two weeks before the important date, he announces that he is planning to be out of town on a fishing trip with the guys. They only go once a year, and this is the traditional weekend. At first, she smiles smugly, trying to keep a straight face, assuming that this is just a clever ruse leading up to a lavish surprise. As the days go on, his act becomes more and more convincing, and finally he leaves on the appointed day with gear, buddies, and beer. He has said that they will celebrate her birthday when he returns, and that unfortunately he will not even be able to call her, since there are no phones where he is going.

At last, her optimism is replaced by blind, cold fury. How dare he leave her alone on her birthday? He clearly doesn't love her. She plans to be gone by the time he and his lousy fish return, but then thinks better of it and decides to stay long enough to give him a piece of her mind and let him know what she thinks of his thoughtless, boorish, insensitive, crude, unloving behavior.

THE BLAME

HE doesn't see the big deal. For years he has gone off with the guys for a males-only weekend, and while he loves her dearly, he's not about to be henpecked in front of the guys. He realizes that she's a bit disappointed, but she didn't seem the least bit upset to begin with, and it's only a week out of their lives, and he does intend to take her out to her favorite restaurant and maybe even get her something extra-special when he returns. What's the problem? She's being childish, clingy, selfish, and possessive. He is absolutely dumbfounded by her coldness and anger when he returns, ready to spend some really fine romantic time with her.

SHE is unconsolable. She has never felt so vulnerable in her whole life. She has been shamed in front of her friends and family, who all want to know her plans for her birthday. She's lied to some and weepingly confided in others, and has seldom felt more miserable. She's not sure that she can ever forgive him sufficiently to get on with the relationship. The man that she has trusted with her heart has humiliated her, ignored her, misled her, and worst of all, chosen time with his friends over time, important time, with her.

THE EXPLANATION

Men and women treat birthdays differently in this society. They are almost always bigger deals for females than males, whether that is because during adolescence

174

girls have girlfriends who organize surprise parties and chart each other's horoscopes and always casually let drop the important date or because women fear aging more and therefore need annual reassurance that they are still loved and lovable. Maybe it even has to do with the relative dependency of girls. They are kept closer to home in general, so birthdays are more often celebrated with Mom's knowledge and assistance, whereas adolescent boys consider the whole thing sissy stuff. Perhaps birthdays are less lavish affairs for males because boys often have smaller groups of friends. A beer with the guys or a ball game will do, or the day can be completely ignored until after the fact. After all, if boys aren't supposed to have feelings, what's the fuss about a birthday?

Having had such different experiences means expectations are going to be worlds apart as well.

THE RESOLUTION

Birthdays are both public and private events. The public aspect is historical: what others did, what they currently do, how they interact and comment. The private part is both how we act and what we want.

The place to begin is with the understanding that birthdays are like the hole in a doughnut—they are defined by the events that surround them. And men and women come from different batters. No matter what either or both decide, the silent (or not so silent) audience here is going to be his friends and her friends as well as his family and her family. That's a lot of pressure on both actors.

The second piece of useful information is that when it comes to difficult, emotional issues that are unspoken because they're hidden or painful (or both), we often mirror—i.e., we act out our wishes. We do for the other person what we wish he or she would do for us. It's great theater but lousy communication. We now have the past and present part of birthdays, the private and public part, the tendency to act out rather than explain, and the difference between how boys and girls, men and women, react to growing older, not to mention the celebration of that act. It's surprising that only the candles are blown out.

To minimize the stress, she needs to figure out what is important to her (*why* is icing on the cake) and then tell him rather than show him. She must, without calling him an inconsiderate lout, explain what her fantasy birthday celebration would be. He needs to communicate his less public and lavish wishes for a quiet night either alone or with the boys without suggesting that she is less important than Larry Bird and the Celtics. Once both have been reassured that they are loved and not weird, what they tell their friends or family or co-workers is less painful or embarrassing. The public nature of birthdays ups the ante, which turns the spotlight on our unresolved questions and insecurities and shakiness. If we've figured out what we want and how to get it, other people's scrutiny is less important.

The first step in getting what you want is to admit what you want, not ask somebody to read your mind— "If you really loved me, you'd know." Reminders along the way a month previous to the birthday are not ill-advised.

Finally, a gift is an attempt to show someone how much you value him or her, but hints are allowed if that someone's imagination is unlikely to match your expectation. How the birthday is celebrated may be the best gift of all.

Free Time

♥

THE GAME

He mentions that he's going to take some time off and relax. She eagerly waits by the phone to hear where they're going. Having not heard from him, she finally gives him a call to find out what's been going on, finds that he's not home, and starts imagining the worst. Days later he calls, relaxed and happy, to see if she wants him to stop by for a couple of hours and tell her how he's spent his time off. She hangs up on him. He figures she's premenstrual and thinks maybe he'll call in a couple of days.

THE BLAME

HE thinks that when she's got her mad face on, it's best to act real dumb, which isn't hard in this particular case. She's the one who's been telling him that he should take some time off and relax, and when he does, she's furious. Who can figure? He decides to just go with the flow and see what happens once she's cooled off, but it's sort of a bummer. Whenever he's happy and relaxed, she seems uptight. No matter what he does, it seems she's never pleased.

SHE can't believe that he would go off and do stuff without her. Going out with the guys occasionally is one thing, but he's always complaining that he never has enough time to spend with her. Great—he finally takes the time and disappears. Maybe their relationship isn't all that important to him after all. If it's not important to him, she sure isn't going to let it be that important to her. He's probably met someone new and is just trying to get rid of her anyway.

THE EXPLANATION

Women treat relationships the way men treat work, and vice versa. When men talk about taking time off, while they may include some time with a woman, for many time off means time off from work, and to many men, relationships are work. Hanging out with the guys, not having to talk or think, and time alone are all very valuable.

To most women, time off means time with their men. While many men are perfectly content to take vacations alone, most women wait for a man to take an "important" trip (often because the man is paying for it, but even if it's dutch).

Vacation time for women is usually meant to consolidate or strengthen a relationship by talking, ironing out problems, seeing where both are going. While both may see sex as a way of coming together and feeling closer, for women, the sex is either the result of working stuff out or the basis and motivation on which the new understanding can be based. For men, it's sex, the more uncomplicated the better. Work is complicated, vacations are simple and comfortable. As women hold significantly more complicated and taxing positions at work and become increasingly comfortable and practical about their own sexuality, this tendency may shift, but it's difficult to reverse eons of acculturation in a decade or so.

THE RESOLUTION

Discussion and scheduling are a partial solution to this problem, but only if she is willing to acknowledge that his first choice of relaxation may not be her. Not that it will be some other woman, but it may be one of the guys, a movie, TV, or even solitude in which he doesn't have to think or talk or please another soul. Once she gets used to this idea, she may not only cut him some slack and not take it quite so personally, but also find that if it works for him, it very well may work for her too. A couple of hours or days or even weeks of being totally self-indulgent and self-sufficient may not only be relaxing, but a real education that provides a fresh perspective. Self-reliance can be a gender-independent commodity that allows time together to be even more valuable.

He may be able to have his cake and eat it by explaining some of his needs and negotiating some ground rules for relaxing time that allows them time together on a less strenuous basis for him. The "if you loved me, you'd . . . know . . . want to spend time with me . . .

care more about my feelings . . . like me better than your friends . . ." makes him feel trapped and her appear clinging, dependent and emotionally childish if not unbalanced. Equality in a relationship means both parties getting their needs expressed on the way to being met by minimizing unspoken concerns on both sides.

Vacations

♥

THE GAME

They never seem to have any real time together, and while nothing seems terribly wrong yet, she feels that something is missing. She has been eagerly looking forward to going away with him since he first mentioned that he was thinking about taking some time off three months ago, but she now believes that the time will truly be a godsend. She has picked a romantic inn, where they can enjoy a candlelight dinner and a romantic walk in the woods. They get to their room, she goes to take a shower and slip into something sexy, and when she returns, he's sprawled out on the bed with all his clothes on fast asleep. She is not amused. The rest of the vacation is downhill from there. They are barely speaking by the time they return home.

THE BLAME

HE views vacations as a time to relax, unwind, catch up on sleep and sex, and let it all hang out. A romantic inn isn't exactly what he had in mind—he prefers sun and surf—but since she had everything planned and her heart was set on the woods, he figured he'd be a nice guy and go along. Just because he fell asleep, well, isn't that what vacations are for anyway?

SHE did all the work, and the least he could have done was to pay *some* attention to her. He was unwilling to talk about any of their problems, treated her like an interruption that had to be tolerated, a nag and an inconvenience, and she had planned everything to be so perfect. She was counting on this vacation to put their relationship back on the fast track, and now everything is a mess.

THE EXPLANATION

She set herself up in two separate ways, at least. First she did all the planning without getting his input. Admittedly, he was willing to sit back and let her do it, but if it's a vacation it should be something that is relaxing and fun for both. In addition, because she did all the planning, she feels he could at least be nice, if not grateful. Once both feel that he has an obligation to be a good guy, it's difficult for either of them to relax. Her taking charge turns out to be a negative for her because of her unrealistic expectations and for him because it makes him feel passive and extraneous. (Many men use a fancy, all-expenses-paid vacation as a kiss-off to a relationship; his paying makes him feel like less of a heel in dumping her, and at least she'll remember the "good time" they had together to soften the blow.) So his relatively powerless role works against her doubly.

Second, she looked to the vacation as a time to work

things out between the two of them, which, to her, means talking. The last thing in the world he wants to do on vacation is talk. He spends every day of his life talking and listening, and what he wants to do on vacation is something different: scuba diving, sleeping, eating, leaving his bed and his mind and his life unmade and unmaid. If he could have his druthers, he'd probably rather go off with the guys, not because they're such great company but because they shut up and leave him alone. He figured the advantage of going away with her was sex, but she's so miffed with him that even that hasn't worked out, and she expects him to dress up in a coat and tie and go someplace fancy for dinner every night too. And then there's the money. He's not sure if he's supposed to pay for everything or if she will feel he's trying to take over. And if she pays for something, is he supposed to be grateful even if he *hates* going to fancy restaurants? He'd thought they really had something going, but this whole thing is ridiculous.

THE RESOLUTION

Vacations are tricky under the best of circumstances because of planning, expectations, who pays, and differing agendas, not to mention things like poison ivy, sunburn, and having to deal with unfamiliar languages and the airlines. Only the most solid relationships can hope to survive vacations. Which begins point number one: if the whole purpose of the vacation is an attempt to patch or redirect a relationship, stay at home and fight it out in the local motel. Vacations, because they involve time and money and travel and expectations, create stress; they don't dispel it until it's almost time to go home.

If two people are bound and determined to go on vacation together, both must be honest about where they would like to go, what they are willing to spend, how they want to dress. This information is best elicited before reservations are made or hearts are set. Both parties can independently and secretly write down a wish list of where, when, how much, etc. and then talk honestly about what they have written after showing the uncensored list to the other.

On vacations as in all things, it is crucial to keep expectations limited and realistic. Travel brochures and tourism bureaus would have you believe it's better where they are, but if it's not good before you leave home, it most likely isn't going to be any better where you're going.

One final thought. If each party pays his or her own way, much of the coercive factor of money disappears. Each is willing to be honest about desires before the trip, since each is putting up his or her own cash, and once there, each can treat the other or not as the spirit moves. In the long run, money is much less important than time, since one we can always get more of and one is quite limited, but in the short run, money can focus issues quite clearly.

Control

THE GAME

They haven't seen each other for several months. She calls him and says she would really like to see him, that it seems that they have some unfinished business. He is delighted to hear from her and tells her so. They agree to have dinner the following week. He suggests their favorite restaurant; she agrees. The morning of the date, he drops off a bottle of expensive perfume at her apartment, sends flowers to her office, and arranges for a limousine to pick her up half an hour before their date. She calls two hours before their date and reschedules for the following week.

THE BLAME

HE feels that she is being manipulative and is playing a game to see how interested he really is. While he is willing to go along, he remembers how everything had to be her way when they were together.

SHE is feeling steamrollered. She called the meeting, and while she is flattered by his attention, he never paid this much attention to her before. She is unsure whether he's setting her up or trying to prove they never should have split or whether once he gets her back, he's going to drop her because he's bored or vengeful. What looked to be a spicy reunion has turned into a tug-of-war.

THE EXPLANATION

There are very few relationships in this life that are based on mutuality and balance. In most, somebody is in control and the other person is forced to respond, whether we're talking about parent/child, employer/employee, or teacher/student. Traditionally, men felt they were in charge of the power issues in relationships, although they have always been intimidated by women's willingness to withhold sex and affection. These days, the roles have been if not reversed, at least muddled, to the extent that power issues are probably among the most complicated, dangerous, and acrimonious. While the desire to gain control is obvious when one is feeling vulnerable, in intimate relationships that grasp for control can increase the person's sense of vulnerability, and the whole process spirals.

She may or may not be trying to exert control over the relationship by calling for a meeting, but his impulse to try to take charge of the circumstances will either cause an escalation of her sense of vulnerability and therefore her need to control or she will simply withdraw. His gestures are disproportionate. It's more than being nice, it's being overwhelmingly nice. Doing too much is expecting too much. If something seems too good to be true, it is.

THE RESOLUTION

Both he and she need to figure out where and why each is feeling vulnerable and how they can instruct the other to minimize the threat, rather than constantly search for control. A battle for control absolutely precludes any chance for ongoing intimacy. Keeping score is the antithesis of trust, security, and ongoing comfort. He needs to admit to himself and to her why he is doing what he is doing and relinquish the control for at least this meeting to her and be willing to negotiate what is obviously an important occasion for both of them. Unless both enjoy unrelenting battle, each has to recognize his or her fear not only of the other, but of loss of control in general, or the reunion is doomed. Real control is control of self and realizing that you can cope with whatever you have to. If you trust your own strength and your partner is unlikely to inflict harm, then control, which is the flip side of a sense of vulnerability in a dangerous situation, will seldom be an issue between the two of you.

Powerful Men and Powerful Women

♥

THE GAME

She is independent, attractive, funny, successful, and sexy, and she hasn't had a date in eight months. Her gay male friends all tell her she is too strong for today's men and threatens the pants off all of them. She wishes that she could figure some way to get the pants off of some even faintly presentable male. What is wrong with men today anyway?

THE BLAME

HE wants a smart, sexy, independent, successful woman as long as she is willing to travel with him when he has a vacation, take time off to raise his kids, understand when he has to spend long hours at work, be forgiving of his occasional indiscretions, and be willing to move if his career dictates. In other words, he wants a terrific woman who is less intelligent, less aggressive, and less successful than he is and willing to pamper him, in return for which he will confer status, material goodies, and affection on her. He feels that there are enough women around who would be pleased with the bargain, so if she's not, he can find someone who is.

SHE wants a coequal relationship in which both are free to pursue independent career goals and come together to enjoy each other's company, minds, bodies, and incomes. She expects him to be an equal in parenting. Housework can be delegated to a housekeeper, since both of them work, and they can either eat out or putter around the kitchen together. She is willing to offer him companionship and a liberating role as a partner rather than forcing him to be a daddy to her little-girlishness.

THE EXPLANATION

We are a society in transition, and while we have allowed women more of a role in the workplace, the home front is relatively impervious to equal-opportunity laws. There have been individual domiciles and male-female pairings for a lot longer than there have been offices to go to and careers to be pursued. The home is an amazingly conservative unit. Many men feel that the gains women have made have been at the expense of the male ego. They are unsure not only of what women want from them but of whether women want them at all; they don't know if there is anything useful they can do or anything they even want to do. Most men do indeed long for the good old days when everybody had a place. Men went out into the cold cruel world and women kept the home fires burning, the meals warm, and the kids under control. Now not only might they lose their jobs to a female who may or may not be competent, but home has been transformed from his castle where his sovereignty was unquestioned to a battlefield where he is only the home-front male and may have to compete for affection.

Her boss can now affirm how wonderful and useful and valuable she is. Her paycheck gives her financial clout, so when she wants him to take time off from his work to take care of the kids or to get home early to help with the meals it's hard to object. She still expects him to be going great guns at work—God knows she is—and to be a superstud at the same time. It's not that she's being unfair or unreasonable, but it's all so new and inconvenient and somehow unmanly. He feels pressured and less in charge and isn't proud of himself for feeling that way.

Since a powerful man can, by definition, have his choice of females, he most often will choose one who makes him feel good about himself and doesn't threaten his masculinity. In most cases this means a woman more powerful than his mother, but considerably less powerful than he is.

Powerful women, laboring under the only standard to which they have been exposed, which is basically the old-fashioned male standard, also naïvely assume that they too are entitled to the choice of the choicest men in society. They quite naturally opt for a powerful man, but one with whom they can be a coequal. That same man is opting for a lesser woman who is willing to defer to his needs. Instant problem.

THE RESOLUTION

This one is a toughy. Societal changes take a long time. When God wanted the Israelites to change their thinking from that of slaves to that of masters, He had them camp out in the desert for forty years. And that's God. Waiting forty years is probably not long enough these days. In Biblical times, forty years comprised two generations, time enough for not only the old ways but the old people to die out. People live longer and write things down these days.

The resolution is not for powerful men to marry younger women who are just starting their careers, for as they become nurtured by the relationship, they too decide that they want what they started out for and are often unwilling to spend their most productive career years at home. So it's a time bomb. Powerful women marrying younger men who are less powerful sets up the same potential for disaster, except that men don't usually stay home with the kids, so child-bearing years are less likely to impact negatively on a man's career.

This may be one of those issues that have to be slogged through on an individual basis, but the real change may have to come with a redefinition of relationships in general—and male and female roles and marriage in particular. It's not even just that marriage has changed, which it has, but that our expectations of what marriage should be have changed. It used to be thought of as a station wagon. It took care of dependent women and children and didn't have to last forever, since men died earlier, 50 percent of women died in childbirth, and many children didn't survive infancy. Now we want relationships to be sports cars: sexy, fast, fun, and focused on the desires rather than basic survival needs of the two adults concerned.

As powerful women become more common, as power is redefined, as relationships and male and female roles are redefined, powerful men and women may or may not be together, but most likely what powerful women are going to have to decide is whether the balancing act is worth the trouble.

Conclusion

♥

Men and women breathe the same air, tread the same ground, but beyond that, there are probably more differences than similarities. While both bleed, their reaction to being wounded, and what wounds them varies as greatly as does what turns them on and off, tires them, excites them.

Please don't be discouraged. If you've absorbed the idea that men and women really do function on a different time schedule, with a different vocabulary, value system, set of priorities and expectations, you've definitely gotten the point of this book. The first point. It may make you feel that any meaningful interaction between the sexes is improbable if not downright impossible. That just means you haven't tuned in to the second message of the book, which is that it is possible to discern the clues, break the code, even predict the situation and the dialogue and, most importantly, change the outcome from one of frustration and hostility to one of compromise and understanding and eventual enlargement of the parameters of our own lives.

A problem can't be solved till its existence is acknowledged. My mom, for one, has been trying to convince me since I was twelve that boys and girls are just the same. She said it when I was too cowardly to invite a boy to a mixer and she meant that rejection feels as rotten to a male as to a female. But that isn't what she said. She said we were just the same, but we're not. (If I had been a slightly more objective observer, I would have noticed that my brothers were not treated the same way as my sisters. They didn't have the same rules, responsibilities, chores, nor were they spoken to in the same tone of voice or even with the same vocabulary. But I was twelve, after all. What do you expect?)

What I expected was that Mom was right.

The Women's Movement encouraged me to continue this benighted belief on a political level. The movement taught that men and women should have equal access to the good (and the bad) things in life, but once you get it into your head that equal means identical, subtleties are going to be lost.

Men and women are DIFFERENT. The differences can be enticing and exciting or excruciating and enraging. It depends on how you view and understand and react to the differences. Now that you know the differences in some very specific and clear ways, with luck you can not only understand how to deal with them (that's what the explanation and resolution sections are all about) but you can foresee, anticipate and perhaps even relish those that are bound to occur in your interactions with the opposite sex.

It has always seemed to me that one of the fun things about sex is that "they" are so different, and in that difference each of us can learn more about self as well as other and expand our understanding of possibilities. Granted, it does take work and concentration and energy, which means that on those days when it would feel better to just kick back and float, things may seem confusing and unfair. But on those days when you're at the top of your form, think of the possibilities. There are men who like and enjoy and appreciate women, and women who are fascinated by and delighted with the differences, and the challenge lies in making the whole greater and smoother and smarter and more effective than the sum of the parts. Hurrah.

For the days in between, a little kindness, a little gentleness, and a heartfelt belief that different is only different, not better or worse, should hold the fort until the struggle to understand can begin again.

Glossary

♥

BOTTLES Another source of sexual dimorphism. Women pour from them; men drink from them. At a bar, this can be disconcerting, but acceptable. When the bottle in question is filled with milk or orange juice and is in a home refrigerator and is replaced empty, this male tendency can result in insult, tears, and sometimes bloodshed.

CAR A male equivalent of a face-lift or a breast implant; a way to regain lost youth, especially the adolescence that never was but should have been.

DIRECTIONS The asking of which is neutral to women and poisonous to men. It is somehow associated with castration, at the very least, hence the difficulty on long trips when women are perfectly willing to stop and inquire about missed turnoffs while men consider the whole thing a TURNOFF. The best compromise is learning to navigate accurately or view trips as adventures.

ESTROGEN POISONING A common but seldom fatal malady that affects women primarily but not exclusively. It results in a tendency to become instantly dependent, passive, and rather silly and to defer to the closest available penis for no particular reason. While it is virulent, its effects tend to wear off once some distance from a penis has been achieved, but many are subject to repeat attacks once a penis resurfaces. The only known cure is heavy and repeated doses of independence, sensibility, and perspective. Women are exceptionally adept at seeing the symptoms of EP in their friends but strangely blind to symptoms in themselves.

EXCITEMENT As in "I wish we had a bit more excitement in our relationship": To a man this is shorthand for oral sex; for a woman it means Friday night at a fancy restaurant. The only thing the two have in common is the same word and use of the same orifice. The opportunity for misunderstanding and hurt feelings and harsh words is unusually high.

HORNY A condition a man assumes will be flattering to a woman, as in "I'm feeling horny . . . let's take a nap," which most women find less than flattering, as in "Go ahead and start without me."

ICE QUEEN SYNDROME, aka BITCH GODDESS, etc. This is the pattern in which a woman plays hard to get and unobtainable until the third date, when she decides the man really does value her, goes to bed with him, and calls the caterer. More often than not, he disappears, not because she is a slut, but because she has set herself up as a challenge. He has also defined her that way (with more than a little urging from her) and now feels that the challenge has been met, and he's off to the next challenge. If she hadn't set it up that way, they might have gotten to know and like each other, but she assumes he is suffering from the PAN, MALE STUD, or PLAYBOY SYNDROME.

INFIDELITY Considered by a man to occur only if he is in *love* with another woman. Considered by a woman to occur if he *looks* at another woman. Another horrible legacy from the "men are only interested in one thing" dictum from all mothers.

KIDS When left over from any earlier marriage, the major cause of the breakup of second marriages for men. Parenting is the hardest job in the world, for which most adults feel totally unprepared. When parents go their different ways and kids are left as hostages to the old relationship they can be used as pawns, surrogate dates, battering rams, distractions, excuses, financial obligations. In short, everything but what they really are, which is confused, angry, often hurt individuals who are torn by a situation not of their choosing or doing. In the midst of the chaos of interactions between men and women, we have to somehow figure out a better way of taking care of the kids. For starters, the best shot they will have at a reasonable adult social/sexual life is if they are raised by BOTH mother and father, with both parents being responsible for nurturance as well as achievement and discipline.

With stepchildren (except VERY young ones and perhaps even then), a stepparent has only two obligations: to be a good host or hostess and a good friend. Discipline can be left to the biological parents.

MEALS The symbolic DMZ left over from childhood where Mom showed love by feeding. Men buy women dinner as an act of nurturance as well as seduction; women ply men with goodies as a shortcut to the heart or heart disease and withhold them as a statement of independence from traditional roles or as a sign of unwillingness to allow gluttony to leave them early widows.

With all this symbolic acting-out going on, it's not surprising that indigestion is at an all-time high and anorexia is a national pastime.

PAN SYNDROME, aka MALE STUD, PLAYBOY, etc. In this common, highly contagious, but treatable malady, the assumption is that any man is always ready to sleep with any woman at any time under any circumstances, whether or not she can fog up a mirror. Unfortunately both men and women are susceptible to believing they have encountered a victim of the syndrome. In men, the recognition causes him to hide his nicer self and act like a hormonally unbalanced teenager who has one night to lose his virginity or turn instantly into a cockroach. In women, an icy exterior is thought to be protective. See ICE QUEEN SYNDROME.

SCARLETT O'HARA SYNDROME Related to, but not identical with, estrogen poisoning. This syndrome can occur at any stage of life but will instantly transport its unfortunate victim (almost always female) to the worst day of her sixteenth year. Common symptoms are sweaty palms, asinine statements, flailing hands, gushing adjectives, batting eyelashes, and an uncontrollable urge to wear ruffles. The symptoms are precipitated by an available male in the near vicinity and can be offset by a couple of dates, a woman friend, or a videotape of her performance. In lieu of these more drastic remedies, the assumption that the object of the performance is gay will often offset the more severe symptoms.

SEXUAL EXPERIMENTATION Most often, when used by a man, a reference to oral sex performed on him by her.

TALK As in "Can we . . .": Words that strike fear and loathing into a man, who figures that what is to follow is (a) a lecture, (b) an attempt to talk him into loving her, (c) tears, or (d) all of the above.

TEARS A substance that terrifies men and liberates women. Men feel that women use tears to gain leverage; women feel men hide any vestige of same as a sign of unmanliness. If she could use less and he could occasionally shed one or two, relationships would be greatly eased.

TESTOSTERONE POISONING A common but seldom fatal malady that affects men primarily but not exclusively. Sufferers feel it necessary to act like overgrown children who must have their way at any cost. Testosterone is especially harmful to insight cells, as has been demonstrated in laboratory tests. You sprinkle testosterone on insight cells in a petri dish and those suckers just shrivel up and die. Susceptibility is engendered early in life and is most often carried by the mother although exacerbated by the father. Sensitivity is a costly but effective cure.

TOILETS A strange arena in which many battles are fought, including, the seat up or down, the door open or closed, or conversations when the throne is occupied. Ranting and raving or shouts of puritanism are less effective than the recognition that men's rooms and ladies' rooms are set up quite differently. (This also explains why women go to the bathroom together and take lots of time exchanging confidences whereas men go alone, keep eyes forward, and don't often chat.)

UNDERSTANDING 1. As in "My wife doesn't understand me": You're lucky, buster; even worse, maybe she does. 2. As in "Why can't you understand me?": This is the role for a mother of a five-year-old. Adults don't ask to be understood, they make themselves understood by understanding their own feelings, conceptualizing them, and communicating them in a clear concise way and then sticking around long enough to make sure they have been communicated and waiting for their partner to make himself or herself understood.

UNDERWEAR Something women try to keep on as long as possible and men want to get off as quickly as possible; in both cases the statements refer to both one's own and the other's. Women want it to be sexy; men in all cases would like to be able to read *The New York Times* through it.

WEDDINGS Something women view as the perfect romantic date, as in "Would you like to be my date for my cousin's wedding?" Men view it as the ultimate date from hell. Both views reflect the perception that it may be contagious.

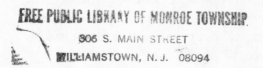

About the Author

♥

Dr. Joy Browne is the host of her own nationally syndicated call-in talk show on ABC Talkradio. She is a licensed clinical psychologist who has taught, been in private practice, and is a regular contributor to local and national television talk shows. She is currently working on a book about rational sex education as well as taking care of elderly parents (separate books), and continues to have a special fondness in her heart for adolescents all evidence to the contrary notwithstanding. This is Dr. Browne's fourth book.